Finding God

Praying the Psalms
in Times of Depression

Thomas Griffith Lewis

Westminster John Knox Press
LOUISVILLE • LONDON

Scripture quotations from the New Revised Standard Version of the Bible are copyright © 1989 by the Division of Christian Education of the National Council of the Churches of Christ in the U.S.A. and are used by permission.

Grateful acknowledgment is made for permission to reprint the following copyrighted material:

Reprinted with permission from *Into Your Hands: Prayers for Times of Depression*, by Michael Hollings and Etta Gullick. Copyright © 1986. Twenty-Third Publications, Mystic, CT 06355.

"Come to the Water," also known as "For Those Tears I Died," by Marsha J. Stevens. Copyright © Bud John Songs, Inc. All rights reserved. Used by permission.

Book design by PerfecType, Nashville, Tennessee
Cover design by Hannus Design

First edition
Published by Westminster John Knox Press
Louisville, Kentucky

This book is printed on acid-free paper that meets the American National Standards Institute Z39.48 standard. ∞

PRINTED IN THE UNITED STATES OF AMERICA

02 03 04 05 06 07 08 09 10 11 — 10 9 8 7 6 5 4 3 2

Library of Congress Cataloging-in-Publication Data
Lewis, Thomas Griffith, date
    Finding God : praying the Psalms in times of depression / by Thomas Griffith Lewis.
        p. cm.
    Includes bibliographical references.
    ISBN 0-664-22573-X (alk. paper)
    1. Depression, Mental—Religious aspects—Christianity. 2. Depressed persons—Religious life. 3. Bible. O.T. Psalms—Criticism, interpretation, etc. I. Title.

BV4910.34 .L49 2002
248.8'625—dc21

                                                                2002022989

To Sebring,
God's special gift

"For surely I know the plans I have for you, says the LORD, plans for your welfare and not for harm, to give you a future with hope. Then when you call upon me and come and pray to me, I will hear you. When you search for me, you will find me."

(Jer. 29:11–13)

Contents

Acknowledgments

I acknowledge the great contributions of Dr. Walter Brueggemann for his work with the psalms of lament. I applied much of his work to depression. Before this was a book, it was a dissertation. In the original work, Dr. Kathleen O'Connor enthusiastically encouraged my work while rigorously testing my biblical assumptions. Dr. Sharon Mook helped clarify the psychological material on depression, and Miriam Moncrief edited, typed, and retyped.

I thank the people God used to help me in my time of depression. Dr. Ben Johnson, my friend and professor, prayed me through. Dr. Laurie Johnson, my counselor, talked me through; Dr. Glen Hittle, my physician, helped me with medication. Sebring, my wife, loved me through the darkest time of my life.

Thanks be to God!

Introduction

Have you ever heard someone say, "I don't know what's wrong with me—I feel depressed"? Or maybe you know someone who cries a lot. Perhaps your friend has lost her zest for life. Maybe she drags around, exhausted. Sleep comes hard. Everything seems to have lost meaning. There is no pleasure in life, only fear, dread, guilt, and heaviness. If this were not bad enough, a darkness hovers over everything and threatens to suffocate life. Do you know anyone who feels that way? Is it depression?

Depression is like an earthquake. Sometimes you only feel a tremor or two—you have a mild brush with depression. Then it moves on. At other times the tremors let you know something big is coming. Sometimes depression hits without warning, causes minor damage, and moves on. But sometimes the despair and darkness settle in. The windows shatter, the foundation cracks, and the house collapses. In its more difficult stages, depression is an illness that is so painful and terrifying that it is almost impossible to understand unless you have experienced it firsthand. At times like this you feel as if the earth has been torn apart and you have fallen into the abyss.

If you are digging out of the wreckage of depression, this book offers hope and help for you.

If you know someone whose life is being wrecked by depression, this book offers a tool to provide hope and help for that person.

If you are a pastor who wants to provide nurture for a depressed person, this book offers help that you can give to them.

The Purpose of This Book

I am writing this book to help people who suffer from depression. Searching for God in the darkness of despair, isolation, and depressed mood is like an animal seeking water in the dry, parched landscape of desert wilderness. To provide a cup of cool water to all who seek is my goal. To help people find God in the despair of their lives is my greatest hope. For that is where hope lies, with the One who created light, who sent light into the world, and in whom there is no darkness:

> If I say, "surely the darkness shall cover me, and the light around me become night," even the darkness is not dark to you (God); the night is as bright as the day, for darkness is as light to you. (Ps. 139:11–13)

I am writing this book because I have experienced the devastation of depression. I know that finding God in the darkness of depression can be the most important source of hope and healing. As a pastor, I always struggle with how much to say about myself. This question plagues me: "Is it helpful or is it exhibitionism?" I have chosen to include my story, not because it is helpful to me (it is), but because my story ties together all the claims this book makes about help for depression. In that sense, my story is only an illustration of one way this illness cripples and how I struggled to get all the help possible. It is an illustration, but it is also a witness. It witnesses to God's faithfulness in finding me at the bottom. I also tell my story, as personal as it is, to try to crack the shell of myth, stigma, and shame that surrounds depression. As I worked on my Doctor of Ministry dissertation on this subject and then this book, people kept asking me what I was writing about. When I told them "depression," they would pause a moment and then tell me a story. It would be a heartbreaking story about someone they know who has depression. My story, I hope, will give permission to others to share their stories.

Who This Book Is For

This book provides resources for three groups: depressed individuals; pastors who want to help depressed persons in their congregations; and mothers, fathers, sisters, brothers, children, and friends who watch someone they love "walk through the darkest valley" (Ps. 23:4a). Help is what all depressed people need. Help comes in many ways: through doctors, through counselors, and through loved ones. This book provides support to shore up the walls of spiritual life, which crumble with the onset of depression. Faith, hope, love, community support, all suffer when depression strikes. The prayers in this book offer easy-to-use approaches to God, the ultimate healer.

How to Use This Book

I suggest four ways to use this book.

One: Use this book for private times of devotional reading. This book is about getting help for depression. The second chapter offers information about how to get help. The last chapter offers spiritual exercises to build our relationship with God through prayer and Scripture. Finding God (who certainly is not lost but almost always seems that way in depression) is the goal. If you are reading this book by yourself, you may want to start a journal. Write your feelings, prayers, responses to Scriptures, and other insights that come to you as you read. You may want to use the questions for reflection at the end of each chapter to help you focus on what depression means to you. The spiritual exercises in the last chapter can be used at random—use whichever speaks to you at the time. Is there someone with whom you can share this journey? It may be a pastor, friend, or family member. It should be someone you trust and feel comfortable with.

Two: Groups may find great help in sharing this book as an exercise. Small church groups, Sunday

School classes (the smaller the better), prayer groups, or special groups that are brought together just for this encounter, all may benefit. I recommend that depressed individuals try to find at least one other person to share this with. Doing so is important because depression causes withdrawal and isolation. The group experience can help overcome withdrawal. It also offers much-needed support.

Three: Pastors and other helping professionals can use this book with depressed people under their care. It is a difficult task to help someone who is suffering from depression. Why is it so difficult? Because of the stigma surrounding depression. People often will not talk about it because of shame or guilt.

Issues of faith enter the picture. If you are a pastor who thinks that *all* the person has to do is pray and have faith, please read this book. Many depressed individuals don't get medical and psychological treatment because they have been taught that faith is all that is required. These people will avoid you and church because they believe their faith is not strong enough or they have sinned and God is punishing them. Pastors can help them see that depression is an illness with medical, psychological, and spiritual components.

If you think someone is depressed, offer this book as information on depression. If appropriate, study the book with them. Or, you may pull together several people for a book study on depression. Remember to include people who want to know more about depression in order to help a spouse, parent, child, or friend.

Four: If you love someone who is depressed, this book may offer you a way to help them. Read it first, then offer it as a gift. If there is a chance to study the book along with the depressed person, this may work even better. Or, help them get into a group. Your depressed friend needs your understanding, support, and guidance, but not judgment, criticism, control, or manipulation. Your friend also needs prayer.

One Last Word Before We Begin

Depression occurs frequently, is extremely complicated, and can be deadly. There are no simple answers or quick cures. All I can do is share the truth I have discovered as one who has been through the illness along with what I have learned from others and point you to the awesome promises of God.

This book encourages holistic help, using *all* the resources available. These include medical, psychological, and spiritual resources.

The book starts with a discussion of depression: what it is, who gets it, how to treat it. Chapter 2 discusses getting help for depression. Next, the book shows how depression damages the spirit. We will examine prayer as a spiritual resource. We will study the ancient prayers of the Hebrew people—the Psalms. There we will discover the great similarity of suffering in people of all ages. The

Psalms provide a way to talk about, think about, and, most importantly, pray about the deep distress of depression. Praying the Psalms helps heal the spiritual hurt of depression. The last chapter provides a guide to praying eight psalms. These spiritual exercises can be used in any order. Each offers a pathway to God through prayer. In the conclusion of the book I discuss how depression can become a gift of grace (you may want to read that first). The appendices offer additional resources to help with depression.

May God bless you as you begin this journey.

CHAPTER 1

Depression

Think about how many people you know who are depressed. You probably know more than one. That's because depression runs rampant today. It is near epidemic proportions. Like a wildfire out of control, depression sweeps through our lives leaving scorched earth behind. It is so frequent today that someone has called depression "the common cold of mental health." If you like numbers, consider this: "The National Institute of Mental Health (NIMH) studies indicate that *clinical* depression strikes 10–20 million Americans each year—one out of four women and one out of 10 men will suffer at least one depressive episode in their lives."[1] These are people with diagnosed *clinical* depression (we'll define this term later). Many Americans, as well as people around the world, suffer from depression that has not been diagnosed and is not

1

clinical depression. It is still real depression causing enormous suffering. That's why, in a recent National Mental Health Association (NMHA) public opinion poll, *half* of American adults reported that they or a family member had suffered from depression at one time or another.[2] Everyone has had a brush with depression, either in themselves or in someone they love. Depression kills, maims, and cripples. It is a serious illness. First, I will define depression.

What Is Depression?

When I speak of depression, I am not talking about a normal mood swing, a bad day, a disappointment, the "blues," or unhappiness. Depression is an illness.

Depression is an illness that affects the way we feel. It has many names, symptoms, and disguises. That makes it difficult to talk about depression, to identify it, and to know what is going on. Some illnesses are easier to identify. Take high blood pressure as an example. The doctor or nurse puts the blood pressure cuff on your arm, inflates it, deflates it, and measures the blood pressure by listening through the stethoscope. If it turns out that your pressure is over a certain level, you have high blood pressure. Then the doctor decides how to treat it. When you go back for checkups, the blood pressure is checked and the treatment is working or not working, depending on the carefully measured pressure. Another example—diabetes: Blood sugar levels can be measured by a simple blood test. It is an objective measurement. The doctor can monitor treatment by the level of blood sugar.

Not so with depression. Feelings are very subjective. They cannot be measured and a number assigned to them. Feelings are difficult to measure because they change frequently. And what seems stressful and painful for one person may be very different for another person. Sometimes you may be physically ill and feel depressed. It's difficult to know whether a loss of energy, one of the symptoms of depression, results from depression or because you have had the flu or an iron deficiency in your body. Depression is so complicated that only professionals are equipped to diagnose it.

Depression is a disorder of the body, mind, and spirit. Depression is identified by the symptoms.

Symptoms of Depression

1. Depressed mood
2. Markedly diminished interest or pleasure
3. Significant weight loss or weight gain or decrease or increase in appetite
4. Insomnia or hypersomnia nearly every day
5. Psychomotor agitation or retardation
6. Fatigue or loss of energy nearly every day
7. Feelings of worthlessness or excessive or inappropriate guilt

8. Diminished ability to think or concentrate, or indecisiveness

9. Recurrent thoughts of death (not just fear of dying)[3]

According to the American Psychiatric Association, you are depressed when you have five or more of the symptoms listed here. And, either depressed mood (1) or diminished interest or pleasure (2) must be present in order to say the problem is depression. In the following pages I will discuss these symptoms.

The first symptom to watch for is depressed mood. When your mood is depressed you feel low, blue, pressed down, a heaviness in your body. This may also include gloominess or "dank joylessness."[4]

William Styron, author of *Sophie's Choice* and other novels, wrote an account of his battle with depression called *Darkness Visible*. Styron does a magnificent job of describing the indescribable pain and symptoms of depression. He describes "gloom crowding in on me, a sense of dread and alienation and, above all, stifling anxiety."[5] During my own time of depression I wrote in my journal, "There is a deadness in all the land." Everything seemed flat, empty, without substance. For me, there were no hills, only flat lands. The "flatness" describes depressed mood.

Another symptom is loss of pleasure or interest. For example, once you loved baseball but now you couldn't care less if you ever saw another game. You are ready to give up your season tickets. In depression almost nothing brings pleasure like it once did. The walk in the park that was once a thrill is now a burden. Depression takes the joy and fun out of life. Food, sex, movies—everything you once enjoyed may lose its appeal. There is little pleasure in life. "My thought processes were being engulfed by a toxic and unnamable tide that obliterated any enjoyable response to the living world."[6] The loss of pleasure drives some depressed individuals to self-medicate on anything that makes them feel better. Alcohol abuse occurs frequently because the depressed person wants to escape pain. As it turns out, the alcohol that first provides a good feeling (euphoria) is dangerous because it actually depresses the central nervous system, making the depression worse. And, although alcohol may help people fall asleep, it disrupts sleep later in the night. If you are depressed, avoid alcohol.

Nothing proves the point about how hard it is to diagnose depression more than the relationship with food. Some depressed people lose their appetite and may drop significant amounts of weight. Others may have an increase in appetite and gain weight. I have always wanted to weigh less than I do. When I became depressed, I thought that at least the consolation prize would be weight loss. No way! I actually gained weight. I ate more and more to try to fill the emptiness inside. Not only does that not work, it adds to the guilt. Also, some of the medications used to treat depression may increase weight gain.

Sleep patterns are like weight gain: They both can move to either extreme. Some depressed people have great difficulty sleeping. They may go to sleep quickly, wake up a short time later, and not be able to get back to sleep. This is one of the most frustrating symptoms of depression. Night after night you lie awake or walk the floor. Soon the loss of sleep leads to exhaustion and fatigue, making daytime dreadful. But equally as disruptive is when you cannot stop sleeping. You seem to sleep your life away, often not being able to work because of hypersomnia. Day and night become confused, making normal functioning almost impossible.

Fatigue or loss of energy that occurs nearly every day is another symptom of depression. This is tied to a slowing down of the nervous system called psychomotor retardation. Everything moves in slow motion. To make things even more confusing, the opposite—agitation—can also occur.

Psychiatrist Dr. Herbert Wagemaker wrote in a recent book that, in his practice, loss of energy seems to be present in every depressed patient. "They are listless, unmotivated, and unable to concentrate. They have been robbed of their ability to enjoy life."[7]

In addition to the above symptoms, depressed individuals may also feel worthless or guilty. The guilt can be out of proportion to anything that has happened in your life. Even when there is no reason for the guilt, it still debilitates. "Of the many dreadful manifestations of the disease, both physical and psychological, a sense of self-hatred or, put less categorically, a failure of self-esteem is one of the most universally experienced symptoms."[8]

Depression upsets the way you think. It becomes difficult to concentrate, make decisions, and think clearly. If you have ever been in a dense fog—surrounded by and engulfed within—you have a sense of what it can be like to think and concentrate when depressed. Everything becomes ghostlike, and it is easy to lose your way in the fog. Fortunately, the fog comes and goes like the fog on the San Francisco Bay. So there are some times when you are more alert than others.

Along with the fog comes "confusion, failure of mental focus and lapse of memory."[9] Depressed people are warned not to make major decisions while they are experiencing the symptoms of depression. There is a good reason for that advice—it may be impossible to make good decisions. With depression, everything becomes distorted. It seems that suddenly and without noticing it, our feelings determine our choices. Clear and logical thinking gives way to these distortions of reality. This loss of clear perspective adds to the decision-making problems. A sure sign that I am slipping back into depression is this distorted negative thinking. It usually goes along with becoming sensitive about small issues. I have learned to recognize this as a warning. Actually, my wife notices it long before I do, and she raises the "red flag" to warn of trouble ahead. Having someone like this who will "speak the truth in love" helps separate facts from illusion. Once you identify the distortion, you can deal with it more effectively.

Death and thoughts of death play heavily on the depressed mind. These also come and go. This is not just a fear of dying but a preoccupation with death. And indeed, depression can lead to suicide.

There are other symptoms of depression. Fear often accompanies depression. Fear of dying, fear of living, fear of vanishing into nothingness, fear of the long sleepless nights, fear of the pain and darkness. Fear of being lost. Fear of losing God.

Pain walks hand in hand with depression. There are two types. Often there is physical pain that may take many different forms. It could be chest pain, stomach pain, or back pain. When checked by medical experts, there is often no apparent cause for the pain. This type of pain hides depression.

Psychic pain is also present. This feels like a broken rib, broken heart, pain when breathing, or an indescribable pain deep in the soul. This type of pain sometimes prevents depressed people from doing one of the best things they can possibly do for themselves—physical exercise. Exercise can help you feel much better.

Depressed people usually withdraw. They withdraw within themselves because they are concerned about survival. They are also fighting against despair and pain. This makes depressed people seem self-focused. Some mistakenly call this self-pity. It is a withdrawal from outside interaction. When seriously depressed, you don't have the energy to carry on a conversation, to get dressed to go out, to buy groceries, or to go to church. Withdrawal has serious consequences. It breaks ties with friends, family, and church at the time when these are most needed. Withdrawal can be a real tip-off that depression lies under the surface.

Restlessness, emptiness, and irritability also occur as symptoms of depression.

Depression is very complicated because the many symptoms are different for each individual. If that were not enough, physical illness masks depression. Sometimes depression coexists with other disorders, which makes it even more difficult to diagnose. There are different levels of severity: mild, moderate, and severe. And there are also different types of depression.

Types of Depression

When most people say, "I'm depressed," they refer to a sadness, discouragement, or blue mood. This may be unhappiness that comes and goes with life. Any number of stresses in life produce this state of mind. Usually it passes as quickly as it came. How do you know if your "blue" mood is unhappiness or depression? The following discussion between a doctor and a depressed person demonstrates the difference between depression and unhappiness.

> "There's a real difference between being unhappy and being depressed," commented one man in therapy. "When my wife and I have an argument, I'm unhappy about it. I don't like it. But it's part of living. We make up in a fairly short time. I may be concerned over it, but I can sleep all right, and I still feel in good spirits. But when I'm depressed, that's a different matter. It hurts all over. It's almost something physical. I can't get to sleep at night, and I can't sleep through the night. Even though there are still times when I'm in pretty good spirits, the mood comes over me nearly every day. It colors the way I look at everything. If my wife and I have a fight, our marriage seems hopeless. If I have a business problem which I would normally react to with some tension and frustration, but which I would deal with promptly and appropriately, I feel as though I'm really a lousy businessman and I battle with the problem of self-confidence instead of just dealing with the issues in front of me."[10]

There is a huge difference between unhappiness, mood swings, and depression.

The first type of depression that we will discuss is called "reactive" or situational depression. This comes as a response to some event in life. Hurt, pain, loss, or stress trigger depressive responses. I mentioned loss because it is frequently a part of depression. Loss takes many forms: loss of a job, a spouse (death or divorce), a pet, friend, a dream, ability to function, money, or possessions. You can even lose your sense of identity—who you believe you are. All these set off powerful emotions. Grief follows loss and has many of the same symptoms as depression. Sadness, loss of interest, turning inward, crying, and feelings of craziness characterize grief. These usually respond to grief counseling and improve over time. We say we feel depressed when we are grieving, but it is different. The difference between grief and depression is this: Grief is a normal pattern of emotions resulting from loss. When prolonged or not dealt with properly, grief may turn into depression. Depression is not a normal emotional response—it is an illness requiring treatment. One of the chief differences is that in depression, we turn against ourselves with self-hatred. In grief, there is much pain and sadness, but it usually does not cause self-rejection like depression does.

Reactive depression can come from loss, stress, personal conflicts, anxiety, violence, and any number of events that hurt us. Reactive depression can be very serious. Recently the story of a young Texas mother who allegedly drowned her five children has gripped the nation. "How could it happen?" we all ask. Postpartum depression has been named as the culprit. The severity of this case makes the point that postpartum depression can be serious business. But Andrea also had major mental illness before the birth of the last baby. Some interesting information has come out in relationship to this story. For example, up to 80 percent of new mothers have some "baby blues." However, between 10 and 20 percent of new mothers experience a full-blown reactive depression.[11] This can require treatment with antidepressant medication. Stress and physiological changes trigger depression in these mothers. This can be a serious depression of the reactive type.

Clinical depression, also called endogenous depression, comes from within. It comes without any obvious outside causes. It may start as a reactive depression and change to clinical depression. In clinical depression, there is an imbalance of chemicals in the brain. These chemicals are called neurotransmitters. When the level of neurotransmitters falls, messages are not transmitted properly within the nervous system. The principal neurotransmitters are dopamine, serotonin, and norepinephrine. When those chemicals are out of balance, all kinds of mood changes occur. Clinical depression is usually treated with antidepressant medications that help restore the normal balance of neurotransmitters.

Endogenous depression can be either unipolar or bipolar. Most people have unipolar depression. This means that the mood swings in one direction: down. Recovery brings it back to normal. Bipolar depression causes enormous mood changes in two directions: depression and mania. In the manic phase of the disease, there is great energy, excitement, animation, and drive.

On the depression side, there is no energy. Other symptoms of depression go along with this phase.

There are other ways to classify depression, including neurotic depression and psychotic depression. Psychotic depression is much more serious and often accompanied by hallucinations or delusions. Cyclothymia is another bipolar depression with much smaller mood swings than manic depression. There is also dsythymia, which is a low-grade depression that lasts over a longer time.

As you can see, there are many types of depression. Sometimes the different types are mixed together. Sometimes depression is hidden by other diseases. Sometimes it is mild, while at other times it can shut down all normal functioning. Depression hurts. It destroys the quality of life. It is also dangerous because of the risk of suicide.

Suicide and Depression

Depression kills. Well, not exactly. Depression leads to suicide in an alarming number of people. The pain of depression leads to the age-old philosophical question, "Is life worth living?" The National Institute of Mental Health reports that in 1997 suicide was the ninth leading cause of death in the United States. When you consider only fifteen- to twenty-four–year-olds, suicide was the third leading cause of death in 1997. Some five hundred thousand people attempt suicide each year.[12]

Furthermore, depression and suicide are closely

linked. Ninety percent of people who kill themselves have depression or another diagnosable mental or substance abuse disorder. The strongest risk factor is depression. Other risk factors are prior suicide attempts, family history of mental or substance abuse disorder, family history of suicide, family violence, firearms in the home, incarceration, and exposure to the suicidal behavior of others including family members, peers, and media reports of suicides.[13]

Women are twice as likely to attempt suicide. But men die from suicide three times as often as women do.[14] The reason is that men use more lethal means of committing suicide. Women are more likely to seek out and receive treatment when in deep despair. Firearms are the most common successful method for both men and women.

Why is suicide so seductive to the person in major depression? Without treatment, suicide becomes more and more of a "way out" of the pain and darkness. Depression causes hopelessness, and the questions "Why do I have to put up with this?", "Why is this happening to me?", and "Is life worth living anymore?" become constant voices within. Guilt, despair, darkness, pain, hopelessness, exhaustion, inability to cope with even simple everyday routines—all add up to a major loss of the will to live. When death seems less painful than life, suicide becomes a real escape route for the depressed person.

If you have a hunch that someone you know is thinking about suicide, take it very seriously. Get your friend to a professional immediately. Or, if you are depressed and thinking of suicide, find someone—a counselor, pastoral counselor, or psychiatrist—and tell them how you feel. Do it right away—don't put it off thinking that these desires to die will go away. They may, but you need someone who can help you whenever thoughts of taking your life creep into your mind. This is serious business. (See appendix A for information on the National Institute of Mental Health.)

Who Gets Depressed?

Almost anybody can. People throughout history have shown signs of depression.

Many biblical figures appeared to suffer from depression. Jeremiah shows indications when he says, "Is it nothing to you, all you who pass by? Look and see if there is any sorrow like my sorrow, which was brought upon me" (Lam. 1:12). Job, Saul, Elijah, Paul, and perhaps even Jesus showed signs of depression.[15] And Hannah (1 Sam. 1:3–20) and Rachel wept for their lost children.

> Through the course of literature and art the theme of depression has run like a durable thread of woe—from Hamlet's soliloquy to the verses of Emily Dickinson and Gerard Mauly Hopkins, from John Donne to

Hawthorne and Dostoyevsky and Poe, Camus and Conrad and Virginia Woolf.[16]

Add to the list Abraham Lincoln and Vincent Van Gogh. In the area of Georgia where I am writing this book, the life of a mountain singer/poet/teacher is celebrated in a summer drama at Young Harris College. This small school lies in the Georgia mountains not a mile from my cabin. Each summer I see again *The Reach of Song* and relive the life of Byron Herbert Reece. Tragically, he ended his life in a dormitory room at the college. The drama shows how the dark clouds of depression built through his life. The changes in his mountain valley, World War II, his rejection by literary critics of the day, and the death of his mother all contributed to his depression. The people of this valley have learned from this tragic story. They refuse to forget.

For Martin Luther, the Protestant reformer of the fifteenth century, depression was a life-long enemy. He once wrote, "I was close to the gates of death and hell."[17] Harry Emerson Fosdick, one of the great preachers of early twentieth-century America, suffered depression. Biographers of Fosdick write of his experience with "a severe neurotic reactive depression" that required a four-month stay in a New York sanitarium. Fosdick called this "the most hideous experience of my life."[18]

James Taylor found his way to fame and fortune in the music world, but not before he was hospitalized for depression at age seventeen. Millions have been touched by his music, including the classic song "Fire and Rain." If you listen closely to the words, you can hear the cry of a person who knows depression. Countless other well-known people throughout history have suffered depression, including composers Peter Tchaikovsky, Wolfgang Amadeus Mozart, and Robert Schumann; authors Ernest Hemingway and F. Scott Fitzgerald; and U.S. president Theodore Roosevelt.

Age and Depression

Depression strikes people of all ages. Research shows that between 7 and 14 percent of children will experience an episode of depression before the age of fifteen. Children and adolescents who have depression are at greater risk for future episodes of depression. Also, depression is three times more common in children whose biological parents suffer from depression, even if the children are raised by parents who do not suffer from depression.

Symptoms in children are much the same as in adults. Children often exhibit irritability as a symptom of depression. They may "act out" their depression more than adults do. This acting out takes the form of temper tantrums, substance abuse, missing school, or even suicide attempts. Children generally respond well to treatment for depression.

Older adults have a high rate of depression. But it simply is not true that all old people are depressed.

Fifteen to 20 percent of people over the age of sixty-five suffer from depression.[19] In older adults, other diseases may complicate depression. Many illnesses may actually cause depression, whereas other illnesses make the diagnosis more difficult. Medications that older adults take can also complicate depression. But older adults usually respond very well to antidepressant therapy.

Other Characteristics

Depression touches almost everyone's life today. If you have not encountered depression firsthand, you may have a relative or friend who knows this dreadful disease intimately. Almost everybody is vulnerable, but your biology and the stressors in your life can make you more vulnerable. "Current research strongly suggests that depression begins with the genes we are born with," writes Susan Dunlap in *Counseling Depressed Women.* "Biology creates the scene. On this stage, there occurs the drama of human life with its joys and pains, delights and losses, loves and hates. The stresses of life can function as triggers to a period of depression, depending on how biologically vulnerable we are."[20]

Some characteristics make people more susceptible to depression. For example, there seems to be a link between depression and powerlessness. Also, depressed individuals tend to see life as negative. Depressed individuals are those who "are generally drawn to the most negative meanings that can conceivably be attributed to events."[21]

Who gets depressed? Almost anyone can. Heredity and life stressors are both involved in complicated ways. Characteristics that seem to be associated with depression are situations of low self-esteem, powerlessness, and a negative view of the world. These are the biological, psychological, and sociological factors.

The Stigma of Depression

One of the big problems with depression comes from the stigma attached to it. Many people won't talk about depression because they are afraid others will mistake depression for weakness, laziness, or failure. I remember talking to a person who was experiencing great difficulty functioning each day. When I suggested to him that depression might be the cause, he quickly responded, "Depression! That's what people have when they don't want to work." It's easy to remain nonchalant and say, "I should be able to control my feelings. All I need to do is work a little harder." This is a natural tendency called *denial*. Some folks numb their feelings with alcohol, television, or drugs. Others may compulsively shop, eat, or work. They are afraid of these bad feelings and hope they will go away. Usually the failure to deal with depression drives it deeper underground. However, one day it will break through, and it might shut everything down.

At the same time, an equally strong force is exerting itself from the outside. Others unconsciously add to the denial by trying to block any discussion of depression.

When I talked to my father about my depression, which was really difficult to do, he tried to understand. He struggled with it, but in the end asked me not to tell others about this illness. Many sufferers have been told the same thing: Keep depression a secret. Here lies a crucial turning point. You must talk about your illness and seek help from all the resources that I will discuss in chapter 2. You must not allow misunderstanding, fear, or shame to keep you from getting the help you need. Depression is not a sign of poor character, weak faith, or bad relationships. It is an illness that requires medical, psychological, and spiritual support.

Conclusion

As you've seen in this chapter, depression is an affective disorder that runs rampant today, impacting millions of Americans either directly or indirectly. Depression is difficult to diagnose, has many symptoms, and can affect almost anyone. But the good news is that depression almost always responds well to treatment. In the next chapter we will look at how to get help for depression.

Questions for Discussion and Reflection

What is depression?

Why is depression such a difficult illness to deal with?

How many types of depression can you name?

Which of them do you think would be the most troubling to live with?

Are some people more likely than others to become depressed? Why?

Name some famous people who have been depressed.

What are some common misunderstandings about depression?

Do you know someone who is depressed?

Have you suffered from depression? What does it feel like? (You may find that it helps to write the answer to this question.)

What is the difference between grief and depression?

๛

CHAPTER 2

Getting Help for Depression

Have you ever been in a troubling situation where all you could do is pray, "Help!"? That is the way it is with depression. In this chapter we will look at what help is available and discuss why the depressed person deserves every resource possible. I share some of my story of struggling with depression to illustrate the different ways to use available resources.

Recognizing the Signs

Today I am writing at a table in our mountain house. When I look out the big window in front of me, I see sunshine on the new leaves of spring. I see new life everywhere as dogwoods bloom, and wildflowers like columbine and trillium put out blossoms. The hosta and ferns of last year begin to send up green shoots. I see birds building nests and hear the shuddering honks of geese as they land in the field behind the house. I see the wind caress the new leaves on the hydrangea and shake the daffodils. But most of all I see light. But there was a time for me when the light went out and darkness reigned.

It was a late, dark night in August when I left the church after a meeting. My wife, Sebring, was a deacon in the church I pastored. She was in this meeting, but we took separate cars home. She left while I closed up the church. On the way home I passed an automobile accident. One of the cars had been hit on the front driver's side and knocked into a deep ditch. Flashing lights were everywhere. "Whew," I thought as they waved me around. When I arrived at my house a few minutes later, I became very confused because Sebring was not there. Where was she? Could she have stopped to see someone? Maybe she stopped at the grocery store. Then it began to come through. That car—could it have been *her* car? Yes, it was the same color. But surely it wasn't her . . . or maybe it was. I turned around and headed back. When I got there, I found her standing on the lawn next to the accident. When I reached her, she was shaking terribly. Her arms and face were covered with blood. The paramedics assured us she had no serious injuries. The windshield and window on her side of the car had exploded into thousands of little pieces of glass, and she had superficial cuts on her arms and face. She had glass in her hair, her eyes, her mouth, and her clothes. I took her to the emergency room, where they treated an abrasion on one eye and cleaned up the cuts. She was frightened and shaken, but she was going to be OK.

I wasn't. It took a while for me to realize it, but all during this incident, I felt *nothing*. No anxiety, no fear, no hurt, no apprehension, no empathy, no anger. Nothing. I was dead inside. Now I knew. I was depressed.

The first sure sign of trouble had come earlier in the year. I was alone in my study praying about a funeral that I had just conducted. Robert Kingsley (name changed) was three years old and had been enrolled in a special program at our church. Robert was not like everyone else; he had spina bifida. Then one night he stopped breathing. His parents were devastated. There was no comfort for them. They were completely without hope. Something about their pain and sense of being totally lost ripped open my soul. I had performed sad funerals before, but never anything like this. In my prayer time the next day I began crying and couldn't stop.

I had recently met a counselor who had just moved to town. We hit it off, and it seemed we were going to have a great friendship. I called Laurie and asked for help. I began counseling in early spring. It was not until the incident with the automobile accident in August that I admitted I was depressed. We had done much work in therapy. Laurie kept coming back to depression, but I would not face the issue. I had known I was troubled, but denied the depression. Now, standing in the emergency room, I knew. Acknowledging it was a turning point. Then I could move on with treatment.

My doctor put me on antidepressant medication. Over the next five years I took four or five of the new antidepressants, each one causing some side effect. I got better, then worse each time I switched. I also continued counseling. This gave me a place to safely explore mountains of stuff that I had never dealt with. I had grown up with the idea that you don't talk about feelings or things that make people uncomfortable. I had never learned how to prioritize my life to take care of my own physical and emotional health. I never permitted myself to grieve the losses in my life. I didn't know how to love myself. I didn't even know that loving myself was an important part of health. It seemed that I pushed hard to do God's work but never thought about how I was part of that work—I had needs, too.

I came to understand depression as an illness that often has an effect on the blood chemistry. The popular term is *chemical imbalance*. This upset in the chemistry of the body leads to a loss of ability to function and distorts your outlook on life. To correct this imbalance sometimes requires trying many different drugs and dosages until you reach an effective dose.

The talk therapy worked at getting me to reconstruct the way I think about things and deal with feelings.

Everything had become distorted, negative, and out of balance. Much of the time I lived in a fog bank, unable to think clearly. Exhaustion was my constant companion. I walked the floor at night and dragged my body through each day, praying for enough energy for Sunday. I also prayed to be able to survive this monster that seemed to be crushing the life out of me. Joy withered. Hope faded. Pain came to stay. The darkness threatened to swallow me up like the whale swallowed Jonah. I feared that my "self" would be lost in it. I have never experienced such sheer misery. I doubted if I would ever have joy again. There were times when I didn't want to live anymore; it didn't seem worth the effort. More than once, I caught myself speeding up and heading my truck toward a bridge abutment. All the while, I tried to keep my problem a secret, thinking that surely if my congregation knew, my ministry would be over.

The most important thing I learned is that you should not try to handle depression alone: You will end up more depressed, and you will flirt with suicide. Finding medical help and moral support can dramatically shorten the depression and help prevent its recurrence. Start with your doctor. Other diseases need to be ruled out before depression can be accurately diagnosed. Ask your doctor to refer you to a licensed counselor or a certified pastoral counselor. Talk with that person and let them help you to move through this difficult time.

Find a friend or pastor who will listen with empathy and who will pray for you and with you. Sometimes a spouse can do this. But often the depression is so overwhelming and threatening that your spouse and others very close to you cannot be good listeners. Remember, they are also going through a major crisis, and they deserve support as well.

When depression strikes, the fuzziness, lack of concentration, indecisiveness, and exhaustion make it difficult to take responsibility for your own health. *But you must.* This will be the fight of your life. You must use every resource available.

Resources for Depression

Resources play a critical role in fighting depression. As a kid, I used to watch a movie about the creature from the black lagoon. This scary monster came up out of the water to capture small children. It was terrifying, because I was a small child. Battling depression is like fighting that creature with your hands tied behind your back.

Resources are the key. Most of us have heard of natural resources. These are the resources found in nature: oil, natural gas, timber, water, air, wildlife, and so on. In a corporation, the personnel department talks about human resources. These are the people who bring their abilities, talents, and gifts to the job. When I talk about resources for fighting depression, there are three major ones: medical, psychological, and spiritual. Resources are also available in family, friends, your own will to survive, church, self-help groups, and others.

MEDICAL RESOURCES

Depression often has a medical component. "Depression is a biological disease," I once heard a young psychiatric resident say. Yes, it's true. Depression is a medical or biological illness. Biology is involved in two ways. We all inherit certain genes that determine our susceptibility to diseases. There is a hereditary component to depression; it often runs in families. Other diseases like cancer and heart disease also have family links. Depression is also a biological illness because the neurotransmitters become depleted.

Medical doctors provide several resources for depression:

1. Physical examination. Your doctor will probably do a complete physical exam before beginning treatment for depression. The reason is simple: Other illnesses can cause the same symptoms as depression. Also, many illnesses mask depression. Your doctor will want to be sure of the diagnosis before beginning treatment.
2. Antidepressant medication. In depression, there is often a chemical imbalance. As mentioned earlier, chemicals in the brain called neurotransmitters act

as chemical messengers. Their job is to relay signals across the gaps in the nerves called *synapses*. When the messengers are in short supply, the signals don't get through, and everything goes awry. Medical doctors, especially psychiatrists, use antidepressant medications to restore the level of depleted neuro-transmitters. If the medicine works, the signals get through again.

Depression, especially clinical depression, may require the use of antidepressants. Today's drugs are generally safe and highly effective. Some have side effects that your doctor will tell you about. Not every drug works for every person. You may have to try more than one before you get the proper help. I tried three or four of the drugs that boost sero-tonin levels, and all caused side effects. Now I take a medication that works on the levels of norepi-nephrine. I have never felt better.

You should know something else about these drugs—it may take several weeks before you start feeling better. Take the medication exactly the way it is prescribed. Don't stop without checking with your doctor.

3. Electro-convulsive treatment. The oldest means of treatment for depression (besides herbal remedies) is electro-convulsive treatment (ECT). In the old days when ECT was used frequently in psychiatric hospitals, it had the image of something used in a

torture chamber. Of course, this was a misunderstanding. The modern version is administered with anesthesia and a muscle relaxant. ECT works by sending an electrical impulse to the brain. This method of treatment provides highly effective results in patients who cannot take medication, those who are suicidal, or those who are unresponsive to other therapy.[1]

4. Psychiatric hospitals. For severe depression, hospitalization may be the best alternative. Your doctor will know about this option and would be the one to arrange for you to go to a hospital. The therapy is more intensive and sometimes can provide relief much more quickly than traditional therapies.

PSYCHOLOGICAL RESOURCES

Psychologists, counselors, and pastoral counselors offer "talk therapy," often called psychotherapy. There are many approaches—cognitive-behavioral, interpersonal, psychodynamic, and others. They all encourage you to explore feelings, attitudes, hurts, and stresses in life. Talking about feelings often leads to new strategies of dealing with hurt and grief. Counseling helps people learn to identify factors that contribute to depression and find new ways to deal with them.[2]

I worked with Laurie, a "cognitive-behavioral" therapist, for several years. These times that we were together were the most difficult work of my life. I learned new ways to deal with all the "stuff" that I had been storing up for years. One of the first things I did was to write down all the losses I had experienced over my lifetime. At first, the list was overwhelming. Then it became clear that I had never adequately grieved these losses. A log-jam of emotions and unmet needs had built up. Slowly we disassembled the logjam, one log at a time. With each new discovery, I had to deal with the feelings and unmet needs that surfaced. The lessons I learned have helped me to have better emotional health today. One thing became clear—medication helps the counseling, and counseling helps the medication. In my case, the two worked together better than either one alone.

Other psychological resources are also helpful. Some psychologists and counselors use group therapy with depression. Art therapy is an emerging discipline that can help the expression of feeling through art.

Spiritual Resources

Depression usually has medical components and psychological components and, therefore, requires medical and psychological help. But what if depression is more than that? What about the spiritual component of depression? Depression fractures the spirit. Hope withers, love dies, faith fades away. Prayer hits an empty sky. Too many times, the depressed person receives medical and/or psychological treatment while the spiritual life is neglected. This book is not about the medical treatment of depression. It is not

about the psychological treatment of depression. It is
about how spiritual resources can be used along with other
resources to provide treatment for the whole person. Let
me tell you a story that may help illustrate the different
resources.

When I was growing up in the South, we had our big
meal of the day at noon. After we had worked all morning, the smells that came from my mother's kitchen
were ecstasy. The scents of cornbread, fried chicken, and
apple pie all wafted on the noon air. It was enough to
make the stomach seem like a black hole and cause your
saliva to flow. On special occasions, usually in the fall,
mother would cook a beef stew. Into the Dutch oven
she would put stew meat, potatoes, carrots, onions, and
bell peppers. The stew bubbled away in a liquid much
like gravy, but thinner. This was the nectar of the gods,
especially when spooned over hot cornbread. Treating
depression is like that stew my mother made. Here's
how: It took all the individual parts to make it just right.
If we say that the meat in the stew is like medical treatment, it is difficult to treat depression without the
"meat." But don't let anyone tell you that meat by itself
makes a stew. If the potatoes represent psychological
treatment, a stew without potatoes would suffer greatly.
Once again, a potato alone is not a stew.

Here is the point: God heals. God is the great physician. God provides doctors, nurses, medicine, psychologists, pastors, and hospitals—everything to heal. God is

the matrix. God is like the beautiful gravy in the stew. The meat and potatoes are in the liquid, and the liquid is in them. The liquid makes all the parts into one whole—into a stew. It is when all the parts are brought together that the whole person is healed.

Today there is a great hunger for God. People seek God in new ways. When I speak of *spiritual,* I refer to the God-given spiritual nature of humans that allows us to be touched by the Spirit of God. "But you are not in the flesh; you are in the Spirit, since the Spirit of God dwells in you" (Rom. 8:9). This book is about using spiritual resources when you are depressed. It will demonstrate how prayer and Scripture can serve as powerful resources, specifically praying the Psalms.

Depression numbs the body, wracks the emotions, and cripples the spirit. Getting better will mean fighting this monster with all the ammunition you can gather. But remember that you are not alone. There will be people to help. God will help. Do you remember the promise from the twenty-third Psalm? "Even though I walk through the darkest valley, I fear no evil; for you are with me; your rod and your staff—they comfort me" (Ps. 23:4).

Depression may be the darkest valley you ever walk through. God does not intend to leave you alone in the dark valley. Instead, God leads you *through* the valley, comforting and supporting as you go.

The Bible uses another vivid image of depression: the pit. God lifts you from the dark and desolate pit:

I waited patiently for the LORD;
    he inclined to me and heard my cry.
He drew me up from the desolate pit,
    out of the miry bog,
And set my feet upon a rock,
    making my steps secure.
He put a new song in my mouth,
    a song of praise to our God.
                 (Ps. 40:1–3a)

Conclusion

Depression has three major components: medical, psychological, and spiritual. Holistic treatment keeps all three in balance by using the resources that each provides. Medical doctors are vitally important in treating depression. So are counselors, psychologists, and pastoral counselors. Often, the spiritual side of depression is ignored. Effective spiritual resources are available to provide help and hope during this serious illness.

It's important to use all the resources available. You must never think you can "tough it out" or "do it on your own." Others can and will help, and the depressed person deserves that support.

As I have said, depression has medical, psychological, and spiritual components. In the next chapter, we will look at depression as a spiritual crisis: Is your cry in vain? Is anybody out there listening?

Questions for Discussion and Reflection

What are the three components of depression?

What are the three main resources for help in depression?

Why is it important to use all three?

Have you ever thought of depression affecting your spirit?

How can a medical doctor help overcome depression?

How can a counselor help battle depression?

What ways can the spirit be nurtured in depression?

What, if anything, stands out about the author's experience with depression?

What can you learn from that?

CHAPTER 3

❧

Depression As a
Spiritual Crisis

Depression is a spiritual crisis of the greatest magnitude.
It devastates the human spirit. "Faith dies, hope withers,
love is impossible, self-loathing is overwhelming."[1]
Although biochemistry and stress are key factors,
depression also causes spiritual problems. In this chapter, we will see how depression has a spiritual side that is
often overlooked in conventional therapy. The spiritual
devastation is most obvious in the loss of hope, death of
faith, loss of self worth, loss of meaning and purpose in
life, loss of community, guilt, sin, and feelings of having
been abandoned by God.

The spiritual dimension of depression is difficult to
describe. Like the Trinity—where God is three in one—
depression is also three in one. It is one disease with
three components: medical, spiritual, and psychological.
Also, like the Trinity, separating the three into neat

compartments seems impossible. All are interrelated, interfacing with each other, affecting each other. Let's look at an example.

I have said that an imbalance of the neurotransmitters in the brain causes all kinds of problems in depression. Much of the more serious depression has this underlying cause. Physical problems like sleep disturbances and loss of energy can be caused by a chemical problem in the brain. Physical problems can also be touched off by emotional stress. Who hasn't lost sleep because they were anxious and worried about something in their life? Lost sleep also causes exhaustion and low energy levels. When you're exhausted, it is difficult to focus on anything else, especially a relationship with God. Both the physical and emotional problems of depression also impact the human spirit and its relationship with God. These are difficult to separate, and each has an influence on the other.

In another example, how can we say whether depression causes a loss of self-worth, or whether low self-worth makes people more vulnerable to depression? How can we separate the medical, emotional, and spiritual? Treatment with medication can lift the depression, and feelings of self-worth will generally improve. Counseling can help people to revise negative attitudes about themselves, which can also improve self-worth.

But I'm not through. Self-rejection that causes the loss of self-worth has a direct impact on the relationship with God. It is, in addition to a medical and psychological problem, a faith problem. Why? Because it destroys the belief that you are created in the image of God and that you are created good. It calls into question your faith in the promise of God to forgive you. God wants you to have abundant life. Jesus said, "I came that they may have life, and have it abundantly" (John 10:10). Depression destroys the abundance of life as it destroys the sense that you are worthwhile. Prayer, faith, Scripture, worship, and sacraments are deep sources of spiritual food. But depression makes prayer difficult, robs you of faith, and makes you withdraw from your community, which deprives you of worship and the Lord's Supper. All of these are ways that God feeds you spiritually. "As a deer longs for flowing streams, so my soul longs for you, O God. My soul thirsts for God, for the living God" (Ps. 42:1–2). Denied access, your life becomes as parched as the desert wilderness.

Depression devastates the life of the spirit. Let's name some of the ways it does that.

Faith

Faith is the gift from God that allows you to stake your claim to the promises of God. In seminary, one of my professors would say, "Faith is counting yourself 'in' on God's promises." Faith is when I realize that grace is mine. It is a gift and a response to the gift. People of God find themselves with faith, but they also struggle to understand and be faithful.

Some people say it's not good to struggle with faith. They would have us believe that healthy faith contains no doubts. But I have discovered that doubt makes faith healthy, resilient, and alive. Doubt pushes faith to new levels of trust in God. To believe and trust God are both parts of what we call faith. As it says in Hebrews 11:1, "Now faith is the assurance of things hoped for, the conviction of things not seen."

In depression, faith may remain strong. But often it withers. When it does, God seems out of the loop. God seems so distant, and the fog makes it hard to believe, especially when everything seems so futile. When you stand in the darkness, the light becomes an unrealistic dream. "You begin to lose your faith in God and yourself. All you can think of is how hopeless your life is."[2] Faith dies. But faith may also lead you out of the wilderness as God rekindles faith.

Hope

Faith and hope are sisters, holding hands with each other. When one goes, so does the other. There once was a sign on a freeway in Los Angeles that said, "Keep Hope Alive." Whether the sign is still there or not, I don't know. But I do know that as you sink into the darkness of depression, it is difficult to keep hope alive. "Hope is a central mark for the Christian faith and depression virtually eliminates the capacity to hope."[3] Why? Part of hope is desire. To hope for something is to desire it with some notion that it will come about. Depression kills desire. And with it goes the hope of getting better, life returning to normal, light breaking through the darkness, and joy. When the connection between hope and faith breaks, hope staggers and falls. "It's hopelessness even more than pain that crushes the soul."[4] God seems to go on vacation, and only darkness remains. Darkness and pain. I wrote in my journal, "I am scattered, without focus and frustrated. Can't get in touch with God this morning—I am aware of an absence—like trying to talk to myself. Hard to praise, gratitude is gone—everything is dead."

Without a community to believe for you, to hope for you, to pray for you, you are lost in the fog. In my times of depression, a small group of people shared the Psalms. These people believed, hoped, and had faith in a God who was there to help the suffering. The Psalms showed me that people have been in trouble since the beginning of history. The Scripture reassured me that others had cried "out of the depths." God heard their cry and gave them new life, a new song, brought them up from the pit, out of the miry bog. Over and over and over the Psalms witness to God's faithfulness to God's people. God promises never to abandon us.

Self-Rejection

In depression, love is impossible—especially love of self. For me, self-love has always been difficult, even though

I was mostly unaware of it. In counseling, I was forced to go back in my life and discover the roots of my self-loathing. I could see a young child seeking, reaching, and grasping for love and attention. My parents were "good" people, people of faith. They were hard-working and committed to their children. But somehow, like many children, I grew up with a deficit of love. And I turned that against myself. All the messages through life that said I was unfit, incompetent, not worthy, and unlovable became swords that I used to attack myself. In the midst of depression, this became an overwhelming problem. I saw everything that came along as proof that I was unworthy of love. My journals are filled with those words. For example, in studying Psalm 22, I wrote in my journal, "All who see me mock at me" (Ps. 22:7a). "No Lord, I mock at myself—and deride and humiliate, and judge harshly—for myself there is no love or peace or reconciliation."

My counselor helped me understand that, in my job as pastor, I poured out understanding, acceptance, and compassion for everyone. Except myself. The story of the Good Samaritan became important to me (Luke 10:29–37). Jesus told this story when he was asked by a student of the Old Testament law about who was his neighbor. Instead of answering the man's questions, Jesus told this story, which is really about how to be a good neighbor. In the story, a man was traveling along the road between Jerusalem and Jericho. Robbers beat and robbed him, and left him for dead on the side of the road. A priest came by and saw the man but kept going. A Levite (like an associate pastor) came by and he, too, saw the man and kept going. Then a Samaritan came by and helped him. He did everything he could, carrying the man to an inn and paying for his recuperation.

Jesus' story had a sharp edge. The priest and Levite were the ones you would expect to help—and they didn't. The Samaritan was the last one the Jews would expect to help—and he did. When we hear a story, we usually identify with one of the characters. Before, when I read this story, I always was the priest who passed by without helping the beaten person. Now, in the struggle with depression, I became the one left on the side of the road. It was not robbers; it was me (and the medical condition) doing it to myself.

There is also a promise here that God doesn't leave the bleeding and battered alongside the road. God sends one with compassion to treat your wounds, to lift and carry you to a safe place where everything needed is provided. That happened for me over the next several years. God sent a doctor, a counselor, and a pastor to help me. But I had to learn how to love myself. (I'm still learning that.) When you reject yourself, you reject God's creation and the promises that God will provide for you. This failure of self-esteem represents the greatest obstacle to spiritual growth. For me, it was the greatest crisis I faced during my bout with depression.

It may also have been the key that unlocked the door to my recovery.

Meaning and Purpose

People of faith are people with a purpose. Purpose gives meaning and makes life significant. God has a purpose for our lives, as this Scripture in Jeremiah 29:11 proclaims: "For surely I know the plans I have for you, says the LORD, plans for your welfare and not for harm."

Depression confuses our purpose. The call to be God's people and to follow God gets lost in the sense of failure and inability to cope. Only something or someone who can show you a bigger picture can help you recover a sense of meaning and purpose. The word "loss" describes depression more than any other: loss of energy; loss of appetite; loss of pleasure; loss of self-worth; loss of ability to concentrate, make decisions, and see clearly; loss of community; loss of meaning and purpose. This loss is spiritual because it affects who you are in relationship to God. During depression, you lose yourself—that is, your real self. The self gives you reasons to live, love, seek happiness, and enjoy a walk in the park. Meaning and purpose slip away as depression distorts your view of self, the world, and your relationship to God and others. In that condition, survival is the only focus. Depressed people often lose their sense of purpose for life. This spiritual problem makes you ask, "What's the use?"

Community

God made people to be in relationships that provide support, love, and a reason to live. Christians believe that God called us to be a part of a special community—the church. Paul called the church the body of Christ (1 Cor. 12:27). In the body, each part has a reason and a purpose. The church gathers to worship and scatters to serve others. Worship may be our most important function in life. When we worship we praise God, give thanks, pray, confess our sins, hear God's Word read and preached, celebrate the sacraments, sing, and receive a blessing. The church unites different people in a special relationship of love, support, and service. Without the community, the spiritual life dries up. Community is the soil of spiritual life.

Depression causes withdrawal. Depressed people feel alienated from others. This causes them to pull away at the time they most need support from others. One reason has to do with focus. Depressed people are usually self-focused. The pain and disability cause a very real preoccupation with your own problems. This self-focus precludes self-giving, which loving relationships require. The loss of energy, the exhaustion, and the unclear thinking all make it almost impossible to be around other people. Being around people drains the last ounce of energy needed for survival. So depression robs the victim of the love and support that might be found in life with others. Withdrawal from the church cuts you off from words of hope and faith that come through worship, especially through the sacraments. When depressed, you need the community to believe when you cannot believe, pray when you can't pray, and hope when hope is gone. Loss of community starves the spirit.

Sin and Guilt

Sin and guilt complicate depression. Sin can be defined as separation from God, a state of brokenness. This state of sin leads to sinful actions or omissions that break God's commandments. In the sense that depression is brokenness and it separates you from God, depression is related to sin. But that is different from the idea that you did something God didn't like, and depression is your punishment. Sometimes depression can be traced to sinful acts that produce guilt. For example, extramarital affairs produce tremendous guilt that can lead to depression. Carrying this around without forgiveness can trigger reactive depression. If something in your life needs to be confessed and forgiven, see your priest, pastor, or rabbi. It is likely that what you experience is false guilt—that is, guilt without a legitimate reason to be guilty. Loss of self-worth can envelope you with shame. Depression distorts the way you see events and the world in general. You blame yourself when the illness may be at fault. If guilt goes along with your depression, seek forgiveness. (See exercise 2.) If you feel steeped in shame, try to see yourself through the loving eyes of God.

Abandonment

Does God abandon God's people? No. Do people with depression *feel* that God has abandoned them? Yes. These feelings of abandonment may result from any number of problems associated with depression: difficulty with prayer, loss of community, feelings of not being worthy of God's love, feelings of guilt, and loss of meaning. These create the perception that God has departed. In Psalm 22:1, the psalm writer says, "My God, my God, why have you forsaken me?" Jesus cried these words from the cross. In the pain of crucifixion, bearing the sin of the world, Jesus felt as if God had abandoned him. God had not abandoned God's Son to this horrible death, yet he felt abandoned. In depression, you feel that you are abandoned. But the promise still stands that God will never abandon us. The apostle Paul reminds us in Romans 8:39, nothing "in all creation will be able to separate us from the love of God in Christ Jesus our Lord."

There is a spiritual condition known as "the Dark Night of the Soul." This is not depression even though it sounds like it. The Dark Night of the Soul has been described by one of the early spiritual fathers of the church, St. John of the Cross. He describes the Dark

Night as a withdrawing of God's presence in order to purify a seeker. The purpose is to generate a deeper spiritual journey—that is, to ultimately bring the person closer to God. Depression and the Dark Night can coexist. With the Dark Night, there is a yearning for God and a seeking that may not be present in the depressed person. But it may. Most of what you encounter is depression, and it carries with it the feeling of abandonment. If you want to know more about the Dark Night, see the book *Dark Night of the Soul* by St. John of the Cross.[5]

Pain

Pain is a spiritual component of depression. Pain? Why pain? Pain is physical. Yes, the pain of a cut or bruise, a broken bone, surgery, or childbirth is physical pain. If you have ever broken a rib, you know how the pain travels throughout your chest.

The pain of depression hurts as bad as a broken rib. It fills your chest with brokenheartedness. It begins with a pain in the soul. It moves to the heart and then into the chest. It hurts to breathe. As Psalm 13:2 puts it, "How long must I bear pain in my soul, and have sorrow in my heart all day long?" "The gray drizzle of horror induced by depression takes on a quality of physical pain."[6] "Depression can be a form of brain pain that is practically unendurable."[7]

When the glaciers cut through Canada and the

northern United States, they gouged out huge craters. Later these craters filled with water and became some of the most beautiful lakes on earth. The pain of depression gouges great craters in our souls. This leaves room for God to make lakes. My counselor kept telling me that pain scooped out space for joy. Perhaps that is so. Certainly some of our greatest joys do originate in our deepest pain. Depression can be a gift that helps you discover God's grace through the healing of old wounds and the birth of a new vision for life.

Love

Why is it impossible to love while depressed? Depression corrodes love for self, seriously damaging the whole network of love. Depression causes a person to withdraw from others. There is no enjoyment in relationships, and relations are built on love. What about the love for God? I believe that continues in depression, although it may seem one-sided. A rich, deep, beautiful relationship with God may become shallow, empty, and dry. But the love of God continues, protected in a cyst that springs back to life when the conditions allow it—when depression lifts. Another difficulty with love lies in the self-focus caused by depression. When you are in the depths of depression, your focus turns inward on yourself. You have nothing to give; the only concern is getting relief. Love requires self-giving, which becomes difficult, if not impossible, in depression.

Family relationships suffer during this time of darkness. Frequently the spouse also becomes depressed. My time of depression was the most difficult time of my life married to Sebring. She worried, became insecure, and perhaps became depressed herself. The gloom spread throughout our household. However, in spite of this, she had the strength to hold it together and keep us afloat until things changed. Love is difficult—if not impossible—during depression. It is critical for loved ones to recognize that depression is an illness, not the consequence of character flaws, laziness, or lack of faith. Depression creates a serious spiritual crisis.

Conclusion

Depression wracks not only the body but also the faith that supports your relationship with God. The person suffering from depression has a crisis of enormous proportions.

You can see the magnitude of the crisis in the way depression devastates the spirit. Faith and hope often disappear. Self-rejection becomes standard. In depression, the meaning and purpose of life become distorted. You cut yourself off from spiritual nourishment when you withdraw from a loving community. Sin, shame, and guilt are prevalent. Pain and the feeling of being abandoned by God haunt the life of the depressed person. Life becomes useless, joyless, and forsaken. Family life suffers, especially when depression is misunderstood.

The good news is that effective treatment, including spiritual help, is readily available. Where do you turn when in deep spiritual trouble? When faith dies and hope withers, is love impossible?[8] Where do you find the nourishment needed to survive while the medication and counseling go to work? You turn to the same spiritual discipline that has sustained people for thousands of years: prayer.

Questions for Discussion and Reflection

What does the author mean by "spiritual"?

How does depression harm the spirit?

Why does faith fade away in depression? What does that mean in your relationship to God?

What is the most painful spiritual effect of depression?

If you know someone who is depressed (or if you are depressed), can you recognize in them these signs of spiritual problems? Which ones? How severe are they? (This may be a good question to write about.)

Does God abandon people when they become depressed?

꒦

CHAPTER 4

Finding God in Prayer

Where do you turn for spiritual help? I have said that chemicals in the brain get out of balance in clinical depression. Medical doctors, especially psychiatrists, help by providing medication. In depression, emotions become distorted and disturbed. Counselors help with that. I have also talked about the spiritual devastation in depression. How do you find help with that? You turn to God.

One of the most amazing events in recent years has been the turning of medicine toward spirituality to ask, "Do religious (spiritual) lifestyles and practices improve healing?" The answers are coming back, "Yes." Some studies have actually attempted to assess the value of prayer. And again, positive results appear. Of course, these studies have many skeptics, as well they should. It is difficult to put prayer and other spiritual practices under the scrutiny of science. So far, Dr. Harold Koenig of Duke University has reported that people who attend religious services have lower levels of interleukin–6, a protein related to immune system diseases.[1]

Koenig has also reported a study of eighty-seven depressed patients who were hospitalized for medical conditions. He found that those with a high degree of religious commitment ("intrinsic religiosity") recovered more quickly from depression.[2] According to Koenig, twelve hundred studies have been done on the healing power of faith and the health effects of spirituality.[3] A survey of healthcare professionals found 94 percent of HMO professionals and 99 percent of family physicians agree that personal prayer can enhance medical treatment. Seventy-five percent of family physicians believe that prayers of others can help promote a patient's recovery.[4] Other studies show that people live longer, recover more quickly, and have a better quality of life when prayer is a part of their life. Once again, remember that prayer undergirds everything else and must never keep you from getting proper medical and/or psychological care.

Our lives are like a journey. We travel through life choosing different paths, hitting bumps in the road, taking detours. Some travel lightly, others carry huge amounts of luggage. Our journey, we hope, brings us closer to God. This means our relationship with God grows richer and deeper. John Bunyon, in *Pilgrim's Progress,* describes the journey to God. Along the way,

Christian (the one on the journey) falls into the "Slough of Despond." To me this represents the pit of depression. What is the way out? For Christian, it was "Help" that came from someplace else:

> Wherefore Christian (The Pilgrim) was left to tumble in the Slough of Despond alone: but still he endeavored to struggle to that side of the slough that was fartherest from his own house, and next to the wicket-gate; the which he did, but could not get out because of the burden that was upon his back: but I beheld in my dream, that a man came to him, whose name was Help, and asked him what he did there:
>
> Christian. "Sir, said Christian, I was bid to go this way . . . And as I was going thither, I fell in here."
>
> Help. "But why did not you look for the steps (the promises)?"
>
> Christian. "Fear followed me so hard that I fled the next way, and fell in."
>
> Help. Then said he, "Give me thine hand:" so he gave him his hand, and he drew him out, Psalm 40:2, and set him upon sound ground, and bid him go on his way.[5]

It is amazing that Bunyon quotes Psalm 40:2: "He drew me up from the desolate pit, out of the miry bog, and set my feet upon a rock." (See spiritual exercise 6.) This is one of the most important Psalms I use to refer to depression. What was the burden on his back that prevented him from being able to climb out of the slough? We each carry burdens. Part of getting through depression is unpacking the burdens and leaving them behind. That's the process of prayer and counseling. But still you need the one called "Help" (God) to lift you—although it may be gradually—from the pit.

Depression saps the energy of life, kills joy, and makes survival the most urgent focus. Tapping into the deep reservoirs of religious faith refocuses energy and offers hope. The symbols of our faith are powerful purveyors of the healing love of God.

> I have heard women say that clinging to a text of scripture, or a line from a hymn or sermon, or simply the memory of a pious grandparent was all the light there was (in depression). Christian beliefs and practices, it is clear, also function to sustain and uphold depressed women.[6]

All of our spiritual practices help. But prayer stands first in line. Prayer is a spiritual resource. It is the way you talk to God and listen to God. Prayer brings you "into God's presence." You can bring your complaints, concerns, and joys to God. You can ask for strength, guidance, and hope. "The great thing is prayer. Prayer itself. If you want a life of prayer, the way to get it is by praying . . . you start where you are and you deepen what you already have."[7] If you think you are depressed, begin with prayer. Pray for God to lead you to the people who can help you. Pray that God will help and give you the strength to get through this illness. If you are too depressed to pray, ask someone to pray for you.

The power of prayer is the connection with God and knowing that God hears, even prays words in and through us. "To be human is to pray, to meditate both day and night on the love and activity of God. We are called to be continuously formed and transformed by the thought (word) of God within us."[8] Most people who have depression think prayer helps.

Why? The answer is both simple and complex. Prayer connects you with God. Most people believe that God can help in depression. That's why so many pray. In prayer, we humans dare to bring our problems, joys, and depression before God. You must remember that prayer is request. When you make a request, it may not be answered the way you intended. God does seem to work on a different timetable than ours. Jesus prayed. In the Bible, the Gospels give a glimpse of Jesus at prayer. He would withdraw to a lonely place and pray. In the Garden of Gethsemane, he prayed that the cup (his imminent suffering and death on the cross) would pass from him. "Not my will but yours be done" (Luke 22:42b) was his prayer. He prayed for strength, for his disciples, and for healing for the sick, blind, and lame. He prayed to be able to do the "will of the Father." Great moments of temptation, struggle, and teaching were supported by his prayers. Jesus also taught his disciples to pray. The Lord's Prayer or "Our Father" prayer provides us with a model:

Our Father who art in heaven, hallowed be thy name.
Thy kingdom come, thy will be done, on earth as it is
   in heaven.
Give us this day our daily bread; and forgive us our
   debts, as we forgive our debtors;
And lead us not into temptation, but deliver us from
   evil.
For thine is the kingdom and the power and the glory,
   forever. Amen.[9]

Jesus taught that we should ask for what we need even
though God already knows our needs. Sometimes our
needs are so deep and so agonizing that our prayers are
like groans that are too deep for words. Everyone who
knows depression knows about groans too deep for words.

Many types of prayer, from the simplest groan to the
more complicated forms of prayer, resonate in the liturgy
of our churches. Here are some different types of prayers:

Adoration—The prayer of adoration attributes to
God praise for who God is.

Thanksgiving—The prayer of thanksgiving praises
God for what God has done. The table prayers we
call "blessing" fall into this category.

Confession—In the prayer of confession, you admit
your sins to God and ask for God's forgiveness.

Petition—The prayer of petition asks God to bless
you—you tell God what your needs are and ask for

help. This may be the most frequent prayer. It can be a prayer for strength, healing, new life.

Intercession—The prayer of intercession occurs when you pray for the needs of others.

There are other forms of prayer, both public and private. For example, the prayer of silence takes place when you empty yourself and listen for God's voice inside. Another example is meditative prayer. In this prayer, you open yourself in silence while meditating on some attribute of God, Scripture, or even an object. This moves you into more of an encounter without words.

Another type of prayer plays the key role in this book: praying Scripture. This is also called *lectio divina*, or divine readings. The spiritual approach in this book will use many of these different prayers, but the major thrust will be praying Scripture—specifically the Psalms of the Old Testament. The prayer for healing is a prayer of petition; that is, you ask God to help you in your time of trouble. Or, if you pray for another, the prayer becomes intercession.

One important distinction to remember—healing and curing may not be the same. As I have said many times, depression has biological, emotional, and spiritual components. Your prayer for healing might include praying for the skills of the medical doctor and counselor. You can pray that God will use the medication to relieve the symptoms of depression.

Spiritual healing may come in another way. It may be the healing of hurtful memories. The counselor helps those emerge. But you can pray for God to heal the wound in your spirit. One doctor has had significant experience with this. She worked on a psychiatric ward and became frustrated because her patients were not getting better. Then she began to pray for them—still using other methods of treatment as well. And remarkable (miraculous) changes started to come about in these previously unresponsive patients. The doctor said this: "What I discovered is that through prayer we can drain those memories (root memories—wounded memories) of their poison through the healing love of Jesus. Once we identify the pain and bring it into the light, Jesus can transform it and free us from its crippling effects."[10]

As you pray a Psalm, you will bring some pain into the light for God to heal. When used this way, the praying of Scripture (*lectio divina*) becomes a prayer for healing. As you read the Scripture, prayers flow from it. The words capture and hold your words. The feelings reflect your feelings; the pain, your pain. This prayer that flows from Scripture is a cry to God.

Balance in life always seems to be the most difficult goal to achieve. This book cries out for a balance in therapy for depression. Wholeness can be achieved by using all the therapeutic resources for depression. Why would you use only part of your arsenal when all of it is needed? Prayer rounds out the treatment for depression.

How do you pray? Prayer is a love relationship with God. In teaching classes on prayer, I have discovered that most people want to know how to pray. The disciples only asked Jesus for one set of instructions: "Lord teach us to pray . . ." (Luke 11:1). Think of prayer as a conversation between you and God. God knows you, but wants you to talk about your joys, hurts, and pain. God wants you to ask for help. The story of blind Bartimaeus makes this point (Mark 10:46–52). Blind Bartimaeus was a beggar who sat by the road in Jericho. Jesus comes by and Bartimaeus cries out as loudly as he can for Jesus to help him. Everyone tells him to be quiet. (That happens with depression.) He yells even louder. Jesus stops and calls for Bartimaeus to come to him. Then a rather strange thing happens. Jesus asks, "What do you want me to do for you?" (Mark 10:51). The man was obviously blind. Did Jesus want Bartimaeus to put his needs into words? Perhaps he wanted blind Bartimaeus to *ask* for what he needed.

God wants you to ask. If you can be completely open and honest, it will help. But when you are depressed, you may not be able to put words together or have the energy to talk or the focus to listen. That's OK. In the spiritual exercises in chapter 6, you will have words to pray. Offer them to God as *your* prayer. Make them personal. Let them speak for you. And don't worry about whether they are the correct words or whether God has heard or even how many times you pray. The phrase "the more the better" is not necessarily true. Oh, by the way, Bartimaeus asked for his sight to return. Jesus told him his faith had made him well, and he could see again. Prayer often opens our "eyes" to see past the debris of our life.

You have heard the old saying that everybody prays in a foxhole. I have always taken that to mean that when danger is imminent, prayer becomes urgent. In my experience with depression, prayer became urgent. I knew no other place to turn. I was doing all the things that were supposed to be done—that is, counseling and taking medication—but somehow I knew that God was my only hope. Sometimes I could not pray—there were no words. Sometimes the sky seemed empty and God seemed an illusion. In those times, others had to pray for me. Later on, I discovered a little book, *Into Your Hands: Prayers for Times of Depression*. Oh, how I wish that I had this book when I needed it most! The authors write, "We know (in depression) something of the 'impossibility' of praying, believing in God, trusting God or seeing any point in anything." They wrote this book to help people pray while depressed:

Yet we also know . . . that even in the darkest tunnel, the most impenetrable fog, and the deepest sense of despair and hopelessness . . . there still is hope even though in despair. . . . We are created out of God's love and he is asking us to take a step forward into the fog, to cling from nothing in our abandonment and open our minds and hearts to one who says, "I have loved you with an everlasting love."[11]

The prayers of these authors are so honest, open, and powerful that I am going to share two of them in hopes they will be helpful to you.

Prayer—that's a joke! At my bleakest moments nothing is possible—one just exists and somehow survives. At other times, the most I can do is to place myself before God and hold out my upturned hands and hold myself out to God—an unspoken "Help!" Somewhere, somehow God must be in the depths but I have yet to find or be found by him there. Yet strangely I would not have it otherwise.[12]

I no longer have any control of my thoughts or somehow even of myself. I am overwhelmed by gloom and am in a well of despair, and I cannot lift myself out of it. I suppose I don't even want to, yet I am miserable beyond belief and remaining in it is unending hell. How can you leave me like this, Lord? I cry to you out of the depth of my despair. Give me some glimpse of hope; lift me up out of the depths; send me the kind of help that will penetrate my gloom, for, Lord, I cannot help myself.[13]

Danger

A spiritual approach to depression has one very real danger. Some people say God heals through prayer alone.

Sometimes that may be true, but this teaching has caused needless suffering by keeping people away from effective medical and psychological therapy. There are many Christians like Andrea. She said, "Well, I prayed and prayed, only it didn't work. I was still depressed. I thought maybe I needed to join a Bible study group to help strengthen my faith. I sort of thought Jesus was testing me and in order to pass the test I had to go it alone."[14] This case illustrates a major misconception about spiritual life and the dangers of "going it alone." I recently talked with a depressed individual who was told by her preacher, "Whatever you do, don't take medication and don't talk to people around here (church) about depression." "Just be faithful" was all the help she received. How many hurting people have been told to keep depression a secret? Doing so blocks the very help the person needs. Seeking wholeness requires that all the possible interventions for depression be considered. Prayer as presented here is the underlying bedrock of all treatment but *never* a substitute for medical and psychological caregivers that God has provided.

Conclusion

To pray is to bring your needs to God and to listen to God. If you pray the way you talk with close friends, you are on the right track. Openness and candor about your needs helps the process. Prayer is request. That means that God is free to respond the way God desires. It may not be what you had in mind, and it may not be according to your timetable. It seems we always want it "now"! Waiting in prayer puts you in God's presence, where you can ask God to intervene. In the meantime, you bask in God's presence.

I talked about several types of prayer, from the groan to the high prayers of the church liturgy. I mentioned praying Scripture (*lectio divina*). This will form the major approach in the spiritual exercises that follow. Praying the prayers of the Bible, the Psalms, will be our strategy.

Questions for Discussion and Reflection

What is prayer?

Name some different types of prayer.

How do they differ?

In your prayer life, what has been most helpful? (This question might be good to write about.)

Which type of prayer listed in this chapter has been part of your prayer life? Why?

What is *lectio divina*? Why is it important in this book?

Have you ever "prayed Scripture"?

What does the story of blind Bartimaeus tell you about relating to Jesus?

What is the role of faith?

Why is it dangerous to keep depression a secret?

CHAPTER 5

Praying the Psalms

Up to this point, it was very quiet. Outside the sun had gone down, and the birds had stopped singing except for the lone cry of the bird of the darkness—the whip-poorwill. Inside the retreat house of the monastery, we huddled in a small bedroom. We were reading psalms. Then someone said to me, "Tom, what psalm would you like to share?" I hesitated, thumbing through my Bible. I stopped at Psalm 130 and we read: "Out of the depths I cry to you, O LORD. Lord, hear my voice!" (Ps. 130:1–2a). Suddenly, I knew that these words from some tormented soul long ago were my words. His cry, my cry. Like the lone bird of the night, I was lifting *my* voice to God. I was depressed. These words became a prayer. They gave me hope. In depression, people of faith often find themselves on their own to ask, "Where is God?"

The Psalms are ancient prayers that the people of Israel used in worship in the Temple. They are part of the Old Testament. The Psalms are prayers and songs written long before Christ. Sometimes we sing a prayer; at other times we pray a song. They are used today in churches, monasteries, public worship, and private devotion. The Psalms are Holy Scripture. God speaks to us through Scripture.

> The Word of Scripture should never stop sounding in your ears and working in you all day long, just like the words of someone you love. And just as you do not analyze the words of someone you love, but accept them as they are said to you, accept the Word of Scripture and ponder it in your heart, as Mary (the mother of Jesus) did. That is all. That is meditation. . . . Do not ask, "How shall I pass this on?" but "What does it say to me?" Then ponder this Word long in your heart until it has gone right into you and taken possession of you.[1]

Because the Psalms are also prayers, we speak to God when we offer them from our hearts. They pull together and amplify our own pain, sorrow, and hurt. The words lift up our words. They do this because the Psalms are poems.

Poems? Who reads poetry anymore? We live in a time when poetry seems outdated. In the age of information, we can communicate huge volumes of information almost instantly. The information we transmit and receive is as precise as possible. Poetry is different. Poetry creates images that might communicate differently to different people. What you hear in poetry may be different than what I hear. This allows the words of poetry to speak to your own experience. When the poem speaks of pain, it may touch your pain of despair and depression. That allows the poem to speak God's word to you while you speak your pain to God, all in the same words.

Also, the images of poetry, like music, touch deep places where "information" never travels. These poetic words touch our deepest feelings, greatest longing, the very essence of our being—our spirit. "Because the psalmists speak poetically, they speak to us—and for us. The deep within them calls out to the deep within us. They articulate the human cry of every person 'out of the depths.' "[2]

With 150 psalms in the Bible, you might expect them to have great differences and similarities. Using the differences and similarities, scholars have divided the Psalms into different types, including story-telling psalms, community and individual laments, penitential psalms, thanksgiving psalms, creation psalms, enthronement psalms, royal psalms, wisdom psalms, trust psalms, and Torah psalms.[3]

Another way of dividing the Psalms has come to us from Walter Brueggemann.[4] He separates them into psalms of orientation, disorientation, and re-orientation. Orientation is the time of well-being in life when everything seems to run smoothly and God is in heaven taking care of things. Disorientation represents the time when life "falls apart, anguished seasons of hurt, alienation, suffering and death."[5] The psalms that reflect these times of dislocation and suffering are the lament psalms. New orientation comes when new life appears. Light comes into the darkness, or joy breaks through despair. It is a new life in many respects. But it is *not* old life—new orientation does not mean going back to the way things used to be. It means forging a new future out of the fire and molten rock. This new life comes as a surprise, a gift from God. It is better than it has ever been before.

Psalms of Lament

Depression disorients. The psalms of lament seem to be a vehicle to carry us through to new light. Keep in mind that the word *lament* means a cry for help from people who have confidence that God will hear their cry. Today the lament serves the same purpose as in ancient Israel— people in trouble cry out to God for help. These prayers come through a faith, although at the time it may not be very obvious, that expects God to do something good in a desperate situation. By praying the laments, you put yourself in a great tradition of people of faith. And that, in itself, is a faith-regenerating event.

Psalms of lament, like personal letters, usually have a specific structure. When you write a letter, you usually put the address at the top along with the date. The salutation follows. The body of the letter makes up the message. The letter ends with, "Sincerely yours." Most letters have those elements. The psalms of lament usually have certain parts, as well. The structure can best be seen in Psalm 13, the shortest of the psalms of lament:

Psalm 13

Prayer for Deliverance from Enemies
To the leader. A Psalm of David.

¹How long, O LORD? Will you forget me forever?
　　How long will you hide your face from me?
²How long must I bear pain in my soul,
　　and have sorrow in my heart all day long?
How long shall my enemy be exalted over me?
³Consider and answer me, O LORD my God!
　　Give light to my eyes, or I will sleep the sleep
　　　of death,
⁴and my enemy will say, "I have prevailed";
　　my foes will rejoice because I am shaken.
⁵But I trusted in your steadfast love;
　　my heart shall rejoice in your salvation.
⁶I will sing to the LORD,
　　because he has dealt bountifully with me.

Now, let's look at structure:

Address—The psalm calls on God. For example, "How long, O LORD" is an address (v. 1).

Complaint—The psalm writer lays out what's wrong. For example, "How long must I bear this pain in my soul, and have sorrow in my heart all day long?" (v. 2).

Petition—The writer asks for God's help. "Consider and answer me, O LORD my God! Give light to my eyes." (v. 3).

Motivations—"I will sleep the sleep of death" (v. 3). The implication is that the writer won't be able to praise God anymore if God lets the psalmist die.

Vengeance—The psalmist asks God to help against enemies (v. 4). This is a reference to not letting the enemy win. A better example comes from Psalm 40:14: "Let all those be put to shame . . . who seek to snatch away my life."

Rejoicing and praise—These words are a radical shift in the mood of the Psalm (vv. 5–6).[6]

The psalm has gone from angry accusation to singing with joy. Amazing, isn't it?

Of course, not every lament has all the parts mentioned above. But the main ingredients are there as complaint turns to rejoicing when the psalm writer pours out his heart to God.[7] The lament psalms are addressed to God in faith and desperation. God is their hope, their only hope.

A mystery lies at the heart of the psalms of lament. A radical change takes place. The psalmist pours out words that are hard and angry or depressed, and suddenly the mood changes to confidence, hope, and trust. What happens? Somehow, God changes despair to hope. Something happens when the writers pray these words.

What happens when the psalm turns from complaint to rejoicing? There are three ideas about this. The first is that by releasing pent-up anger, hurt, frustration, and pain, the psalmist is relieved and feels better. Another idea is that in the temple worship, a priest announced forgiveness or healing from the trouble expressed, and then the psalm turned to joy because the worshiper heard the promise of God. The third idea, and for me the most important, claims that God intervenes to bring healing and hope. We can't discount any of these. But for the person with depression who prays these psalms, the reassurance that others have felt the same pain and hopelessness means something. And to put in words the trouble of your own soul releases the pent-up anger and hurt. This begins the healing. But most important, when you pray, asking God for help, God heals. The healing may not come every time or in every way that you have in mind, but putting it in God's care with expectation releases the burden and invites healing.

Many of the psalms that follow will touch on intense feelings. If that is where the words lead you, it's OK. Whatever you feel—anger, despair, loss of energy, inability to eat or sleep, inability to stop eating or sleeping, unforgiveness, exhaustion, or guilt—these have been felt before by someone who brought those feelings to God in prayer. Try to be honest about your feelings and express them in prayer. God will not be shocked or disgusted by your feelings and struggles.

In the pit of my depression, I met with one or two other pastors. We prayed the Psalms together. We also listened to each other and prayed for what we heard. We each had our favorite psalm. Mine was Psalm 130. Each time we gathered, I prayed, "Out of the depths I cry to you, O LORD. Lord, hear my voice!" Somehow, I knew that in the depths I would find God, or better yet, God would find me. In the deepest hurt of our life, we find the greatest grace. At times during the depths of depression, I was somehow closer to God than ever before or since. Like a homeless person wandering the desolate city streets, I was completely dependent on grace—without it, I knew I would die. Through these times of praying the Psalms, God provided for me.

1. The Psalms described my condition. That meant that others before me understood what I was going through. God understood. That helped me know that my trouble was real.

2. Praying the Psalms turned me again and again toward God for whatever hope I could receive. Forgiveness was very important to me.

3. Praying with others provided a community and pulled me "outside myself." The community

provided a concrete experience of God's love and acceptance.

4. God heard my cry and over time pulled me up from the depths and put a new song in my heart.

As part of my getting better, I could sing new songs and pray new Psalms—ones of joy and devotion, worship and praise. It was also during this time of emerging from the darkness that I renewed my baptismal vows. This was a marker event for me. It was my way of saying, "Thank you God. You were faithful. I dedicate my life to you."

Conclusion

The Psalms speak for us and to us. They are helpful as prayers in depression. Because these ancient songs and prayers are written in poetry, their words have the ability to capture and hold your words. It is not important whether the psalm writers suffered from clinical depression as we know it today. Their words of pain, darkness, desperation, and abandonment can touch those same feelings in you. They felt like you feel. And they spoke those feelings with hope and faith that God would come to their rescue. You can speak their words to God on your own behalf. And, somehow, somewhere in the mystery of it all, God helps. Our tears of sorrow turn to songs of praise.

Questions for Discussion and Reflection

What are psalms? Where are they found?

What are some characteristics of psalms?

Can you name different types of psalms?

What is orientation, disorientation, and new orientation? What do those words mean? What have they to do with psalms?

When you think about your life, can you see times of orientation? Disorientation? New orientation? Where does depression fit in this description?

What is a lament? What is its purpose? Can you name some different parts of a psalm of lament?

What is the miracle that happens in a psalm of lament? What happens and why?

❧

CHAPTER 6

Spiritual Exercises

I have said that depression is an illness that devastates the mind, body, and spirit. Effective treatment uses all the resources available: medical, psychological, and spiritual. In the area of spiritual help, prayer has profound effects upon healing—not as a substitute for other types of therapy, but as a supplement. This chapter contains a series of spiritual exercises to help you use the Psalms as resources for prayer in times of depression.

There are six psalms of lament: Psalms 13, 130, 22, 42–43, 77, and 40. (Psalms 42 and 43 are considered as one.) I have also included a psalm of new orientation (30) and a psalm of confidence (131). These are filled with new hope, joy, and life. Each psalm has been selected for the ways it might speak to someone who is depressed. Each exercise has instructions to lead you through. These exercises are certainly not limited to people with depression. They are words of hope for anyone who is troubled. These spiritual exercises may be helpful in any degree of depression, from the sadness of a bad day to more serious cases of clinical depression.

Here are some suggestions for using these spiritual exercises:

1. Find a quiet spot where you can spend some time without interruption.

2. Invite another friend or your pastor to join you in these prayers. Select one of the exercises.

3. Begin with the prayer for God to clear your mind and settle your emotions. Pray for God to open your heart to receive what God has for you.

4. Thank God for your life, even if it's a mess.

5. Select and read one of the psalms in this guide. Read it prayerfully. It may help to read it out loud. If you are in a group, share the readings.

6. As you pray the words of the psalm, listen for any phrases or words that seem very important. Dwell on those for a while. What are they saying to you? What are they telling you about God, your condition, or your life? Are the words inviting you to do something or take another step in getting better?

7. Share what you discover with the people praying with you. Listen to their responses. Don't be

discouraged if nothing touches you at first.
Depression makes it hard to pray. Just keep at it.

8. You may want to write what you hear, the way you feel, and any prayers that come to you. A simple spiral notebook works fine to keep track of what you write.

9. End with a prayer for each other or for what you heard in the psalm. Thank God for the promise of new life. If you find it hard to pray, you may use one of the hymns and spiritual songs that are included. I hope you will be inspired by the words and offer them as prayers when you have no words of your own.

EXERCISE 1

PSALM 13: "HOW LONG, O LORD?"

BEFORE YOU BEGIN

Psalm 13 teaches you how to pray. It also helps you release feelings of frustration and anger. The writer apparently suffers great distress and anxiety. Psalm 13 begins with protest, asks God for help, and ends in praise. This prayer shows you how to be honest with your feelings, taking them to God and expecting help.

BEGIN WITH PRAYER

Here is a suggested prayer.

> Merciful God, I come to you today filled with feelings
> that I don't know how to handle. Can you handle them,
> O God? I know you can. I am so tired of waiting for this
> depression to get better. Will you come and help me?
> Help me, please. I thank you, O God, for my life, even
> with the mess it's in. Speak to the deep hurts in my life
> and let me see your light. Amen.

READ THE PSALM

Find a place that is quiet. It is almost always better for
depressed people to pray in a group. Try to find someone with whom to share this experience. It could be your
spouse, your pastor, a friend, or a small group of people.
If you are alone, try praying out loud. If in a group, share
the readings. Pray the words slowly and reverently. Let all
your senses be open to God. What do you hear? Does a
special word stand out? If so, think about that word for
a while, and then move on. Since this psalm is short, you
will probably want to pray all the verses. Pray it again. Do
any words speak to you about your life, your depression,
or your feelings? Stay with them for a while. Read the
psalm through again and ask if these words hold an invitation for you. What is God calling you to do or be? Is
God offering you a new perspective on life?

Psalm 13

Prayer for Deliverance from Enemies
To the leader. A Psalm of David.

¹How long, O LORD? Will you forget me forever?
How long will you hide your face from me?
²How long must I bear pain in my soul,
and have sorrow in my heart all day long?
How long shall my enemy be exalted over me?

³Consider and answer me, O LORD my God!
Give light to my eyes, or I will sleep the sleep
of death,
⁴and my enemy will say, "I have prevailed";
my foes will rejoice because I am shaken.

⁵But I trusted in your steadfast love;
my heart shall rejoice in your salvation.
⁶I will sing to the LORD,
because he has dealt bountifully with me.

COMMENTS

This prayer begins with protest. It's OK to protest, rage, and even shake your fist at God. You need help with the suffering. You may not know how much hurt you have endured until you say the words of this psalm. After the angry protest, the psalmist asks for help. Only then can the prayer turn to praise.

When you pray, "How long, O Lord?" can you feel yourself getting fed up and impatient with suffering?

These words may touch deep feelings in you. "How long, O Lord? How long, O Lord? Will you forget me forever? How long must I bear this pain in my soul? How long must I wallow in sorrow and soak up this near-death experience? Will it last forever? Is there no hope for me to feel better?"

What is it that causes you to cry out, "How long, O Lord?" Depression devastates the spirit and is like death in some ways. Darkness gathers. With it comes that terrible fear that nothing will survive. Depression causes pain and destruction to your inner life and well-being. It may be time to cry out, "How long?"

If you have never experienced the more troubling types of depression, it is impossible to understand the pain involved. It begins with psychic pain. Then it moves into your chest and feels like a broken heart. Sometimes it becomes a physical pain. It is real and indescribable. "The incomprehension has usually been due to the basic inability of healthy people to imagine a form of torment so alien to everyday experience. For myself, the pain is most closely connected to drowning or suffocation."[1] "How long must I bear pain in my soul?" Could the psalmist be talking about the pain of depression?

When I was in a lot of pain from depression, I discovered something that became very important to me: a crucifix. In my tradition (Presbyterian), the crosses we use in worship are empty—that is, the body of Jesus is not there. The empty cross signifies the resurrection. In other traditions, the body of Jesus remains on the cross. His broken and bleeding body reminds us of his suffering. I bought such a crucifix and put it in my desk drawer. When I felt awful, I took it out and studied it. I realized two things: (1) Jesus suffered for me, and (2) Jesus is suffering with me as I suffer. I suppose I had always known that, but somehow the truth of his suffering hit me at a deeper level than ever before. The result was a bittersweet gratitude that usually ended in a prayer of thanksgiving and cry for release.

The psalm mentions an enemy. Who is the enemy in depression? Who is your enemy? My enemy always seemed to be despair. Despair drags you down into the pit. Despair tells you to give up—that there is no hope. Despair distorts reality. Fight despair. Don't let it win. Despair is not what made you feel so bad; it's what keeps you feeling bad. How do you fight despair? Turn to God. That's where hope resides. Trust. Decide you will not let despair conquer you.

There is a pause after verse 4. It is a time of waiting. How long is the wait? Sometimes it seems forever. At other times, letting the rage go speeds up the process and the wait is not so long. When you pray this psalm, wait. In depression, we wait for the feelings to change, for the therapy to work, for God to heal. In your waiting, try to believe that light is already breaking through the darkness. Joy and singing may lie ahead.

You may discover that something mysterious and wonderful is happening in your depression. Words of trust may emerge where doubt and anger lay before. It may happen as you remember how you once trusted God: "I trusted in your steadfast love; my heart shall rejoice in your salvation. I will sing to the LORD, because he has dealt bountifully with me" (Ps. 13:5–6). For the psalmist, God is in the midst of the trouble and is the only hope for relief. You are not in this by yourself. Hope in God. It's incredible—the psalm takes you from rage to singing. Read, looking for a word or phrase that grabs you. "How long, O LORD?" You hear that phrase over and over. What is it saying about your life? Is it inviting you to take a step, to do something different?

DISCUSSION AND WRITING

If you are in a group, let each person have an opportunity to say what they heard from Psalm 13. What are the different ways that people heard the words of the psalm? How did God use the words to speak to your particular situation?

Martin Luther said about Psalm 13, "Hope despairs and despair hopes at the same time."[2] What does that mean to you?

While the words are still fresh in your mind, try writing what you heard, how it affected you, and what else you want to think about. Sometimes I write my prayers in a journal or use the outline of the psalm to write my own psalm. Take some time to reflect.

FINISHING

Close with prayer. In your prayer, thank God for the time together (if in a group), for the insight, and for any encouragement you received or any ways you are feeling hopeful. It is appropriate to ask God to help you and the members of your group. Ask for healing—be specific about your needs and desires. Most of all, ask God to give you strength to fight the depression. Pray for others with depression. Pray for those who live with someone who is depressed. Here is an example:

> Thank you God. Help me to know you are always with me. Thank you for hearing how angry and sad I am. Help me through the dark times. Give me your love. Amen.

Conclude with the Lord's Prayer or the words to a favorite hymn.

EXERCISE 2

PSALM 130: "OUT OF THE DEPTHS"

BEFORE YOU BEGIN

Psalm 130 is another lament. People through the ages have identified with the words "out of the depths." This psalm is from an individual who pleads for deliverance from sin, which is the trouble that put him in the depths. He asks God for forgiveness. He reassures Israel that patient prayer during his nightlong vigils results in forgiveness of sin. This psalm contains good news—God forgives us.

<small>BEGIN WITH PRAYER</small>

> Merciful God, I come to you today with burdens too heavy to carry. I know that you will help me. I have sinned against you and ones I love. I seek your forgiveness. Please lift me out of the gloom and darkness that suffocate me. Help me, O God. Amen.

<small>READ THE PSALM</small>

As you read Psalm 130, listen for words or phrases that stand out to you. Read it more than once. Do the same words stand out each time? When you read the psalm, remember that this prayer speaks your words to God. It is also Scripture that speaks God's words to you. Is God telling you something about your life? Is God showing you a new way to deal with sin, guilt, and depression? Listen for words of assurance that sins confessed are sins forgiven.

Psalm 130
Waiting for Divine Redemption
A Song of Ascents.

¹Out of the depths I cry to you, O LORD.
  ²Lord, hear my voice!
Let your ears be attentive to the voice of my
  supplications!

³If you, O LORD, should mark iniquities,
  Lord, who could stand?
⁴But there is forgiveness with you,
  so that you may be revered.

⁵I wait for the LORD, my soul waits,
  and in his word I hope;
⁶my soul waits for the Lord
  more than those who watch for the morning.

⁷O Israel, hope in the LORD!
  For with the LORD there is steadfast love,
  and with him is great power to redeem.
⁸It is he who will redeem Israel
  from all its iniquities.

<u>COMMENTS</u>

I prayed Psalm 130 over and over during my time of depression. The psalm begins with the words, "Out of the depths . . ." When you are depressed, you know the meaning of this word "depths." The depths signify drowning in distress, being overwhelmed and sucked down by the bottomless waters of trouble.[3]

In the movie, *The Piano,* there is a scene when Holly Hunter's character is leaving the island where she had come to marry. The marriage had been disastrous. Now she leaves with her piano—her only way of expressing herself, since she was mute. The piano has served as her words, expressions of feelings, and communications. It also had led her into an extramarital affair that ended her marriage and sent her away from the island. The piano is very large and the boat small. The danger of capsizing becomes very real, so she orders them to throw the piano overboard. As it sinks into the depths of the ocean, a rope attached to it uncoils. She puts her foot in the middle of the coil, the rope wraps around one of her high-top shoes, and she is pulled into the ocean. It's not clear why she deliberately attached herself to the sinking piano—perhaps she could not bear to be separated from it or perhaps she wanted to join it in the cold ocean grave. After a few moments she frees herself from the rope by kicking off the high-topped shoe. She emerges from the water a new person—one determined to live, not die.

No one deliberately chooses depression. There may be things to which we are attached that pull us under— into the depths. These could be attitudes, a distorted view of life, despair, apathy, or sin. We have to kick loose from these "pianos" that pull us under. God wants to help with that. Prayer provides access to the One who does not count our iniquities against us but provides forgiveness instead. We must choose to live by trusting in God.

The people of Israel understood that their problem was sin. They were helpless to be faithful to God. They broke their relationship with God over and over. Their only hope was that God would do what they could not do—forgive them. Today we understand illness in different ways. We know more about chemicals in the brain that cause depression and a feeling of guilt that comes for no reason at all. God does not punish people by making them depressed. However, there may be a time when you feel that unresolved sin or the effects of evil in your life may be some element of depression. If so, hear the promise of this psalm—if God added up all our sins, we would all be doomed. But God forgives us, erasing the sin. Is it too good to be true? It seems that way. But there is hope in God's promise of forgiveness.

The key is to wait and watch. For most of us, waiting and watching seems like we are doing nothing. Waiting for God is sometimes like those watchmen waiting through the night. If you are depressed, you may wait through sleepless nights. Someone said that depression is when everything seems like three o'clock in the morning. Three o'clock in the morning is terrifying. You can't sleep. All you can do is worry. At three o'clock in the morning, everything seems hopeless. With the dawn comes another change, and the fears of the night melt away. The psalmist is saying to wait for the Lord the same way you wait out that sleepless night. Pray and wait. As depression lifts, the wait seems to be over. There is Good News: "Hope in the Lord."

DISCUSSION AND WRITING

What did you hear? Why is it important to you? If you are in a group, share what was important to each person in Psalm 130. You may want to write what you heard and what it means to you. Write out your prayer to God. Keep in mind that sometimes you don't hear anything. But later an insight may come to you quietly and secretly. If you are keeping a journal, you may want to stop now and write any insights you have received.

FINISHING

Sometimes the words of a familiar hymn can express what you cannot express in words. At these times, you can offer the words of the hymn as a prayer.

EXERCISE 3

PSALM 22: "WHY HAVE YOU FORSAKEN ME?"

BEFORE YOU BEGIN

This psalm of lament begins with the same words Jesus cried from the cross. They represented his feeling of being forsaken. Often in depression, you may feel forsaken and abandoned by God. The psalm moves from those gripping words to asking for help. The psalm writer has trouble with enemies. The psalm concludes with praise, shouts of confidence, and thanksgiving. This psalm is long. You may want to break it into pieces. Verses 1–11 could be one prayer, 12–21 another, and 22–31 another.

BEGIN WITH PRAYER

Lord, did you ever meet people burdened by depression when you were on the earth? Was the man who was possessed by devils depressed like me? Some deep force I don't want drags me down into a gulf of misery. A black cloud surrounds me. I can't escape. There is no way out, and it seems hopeless. Was your darkness on the cross like this? Lift me out of the depths. Say, "Peace; be still," in such a way as to stop the blackness that buries me. Lay your cool hand on my brow and say, "Be whole again." Heal me, Lord, cast out my fears, my devils, my darkness. Save me, Lord, save me! Amen.[4]

READ THE PSALM

Read Psalm 22 all the way through. Then go back to the parts that spoke to you. Spend time with those words and verses. Be sure to hear the ending that offers confidence in God to deliver from all enemies. You could also break the psalm into sections as suggested above. Let the words touch your heart. Bathe in them; soak up the promises, drain off the hurt.

Psalm 22

Plea for Deliverance from Suffering and Hostility

To the leader: according to The Deer of the Dawn.

A Psalm of David.

¹My God, my God, why have you forsaken me?
  Why are you so far from helping me, from the words
    of my groaning?
²O my God, I cry by day, but you do not answer;
  and by night, but find no rest.
³Yet you are holy,
  enthroned on the praises of Israel.
⁴In you our ancestors trusted;
  they trusted, and you delivered them.
⁵To you they cried, and were saved;
  in you they trusted, and were not put to shame.

⁶But I am a worm, and not human;
  scorned by others, and despised by the people.
⁷All who see me mock at me;
  they make mouths at me, they shake their heads;
⁸"Commit your cause to the LORD; let him deliver—
  let him rescue the one in whom he delights!"

⁹Yet it was you who took me from the womb;
  you kept me safe on my mother's breast.
¹⁰On you I was cast from my birth,
  and since my mother bore me you have been
    my God.
¹¹Do not be far from me,
  for trouble is near
  and there is no one to help.

¹²Many bulls encircle me,
 strong bulls of Bāʹshan surround me;
¹³they open wide their mouths at me,
 like a ravening and roaring lion.

¹⁴I am poured out like water,
 and all my bones are out of joint;
my heart is like wax;
 it is melted within my breast;
¹⁵my mouth is dried up like a potsherd,
 and my tongue sticks to my jaws;
 you lay me in the dust of death.

¹⁶For dogs are all around me;
 a company of evildoers encircles me.
My hands and feet have shriveled;
¹⁷I can count all my bones.
They stare and gloat over me;
¹⁸they divide my clothes among themselves,
 and for my clothing they cast lots.

¹⁹But you, O LORD, do not be far away!
 O my help, come quickly to my aid!
²⁰Deliver my soul from the sword,
 my life from the power of the dog!
 ²¹Save me from the mouth of the lion!
From the horns of the wild oxen you have rescued me.
²²I will tell of your name to my brothers and sisters;
 in the midst of the congregation I will praise you;
²³You who fear the LORD, praise him!
 All you offspring of Jacob, glorify him;
 stand in awe of him, all you offspring of Israel!

²⁴For he did not despise or abhor
    the affliction of the afflicted;
he did not hide his face from me,
    but heard when I cried to him.

²⁵From you comes my praise in the great congregation;
    my vows I will pay before those who fear him.
²⁶The poor shall eat and be satisfied;
    those who seek him shall praise the LORD.
    May your hearts live forever!

²⁷All the ends of the earth shall remember
    and turn to the LORD;
and all the families of the nations
    shall worship before him.
²⁸For dominion belongs to the LORD,
    and he rules over the nations.
²⁹To him, indeed, shall all who sleep in the earth
      bow down;
before him shall bow all who go down
      to the dust,
    and I shall live for him.
³⁰Posterity will serve him;
    future generations will be told about the Lord,
³¹and proclaim his deliverance to a people yet unborn,
    saying that he has done it.

COMMENTS

You may recognize verse 1, "My God, my God, why have you forsaken me?" These are the words Jesus prayed from the cross. Jesus felt abandoned by God. Is it any wonder that in depression there are times when we too feel abandoned, alone, and lost? This is a spiritual crisis.

Sometimes prayer doesn't seem to work. You may feel cut off from God. "I cry by day, but you do not answer; and by night, but find no rest" (v. 2). There is no rest in depression.

Remembering how God has helped in the past renews your trust. Try making a list of the ways God has been there for you in your life. You may find that doing so will help you to trust God now. List all the important people in your life who have loved you. List the pastors who have touched your life. List the ways God has blessed you, even in pain. What about the ways God has taken a mistake and made good come from it? As you remember, you'll grow in gratitude and faith. If God has been there before, God will continue to be faithful.

Depression produces self-rejection and self-hatred. Nothing is more disturbing. In verse 6, the psalm writer says, "I am a worm." Have you ever thought of yourself as a worm? A worm has no spine. Perhaps you felt this way when you were not strong enough to stand up to problems or enemies. Depression robs you of the strength to stand up, sit up, or even live. Exhaustion makes you feel like a worm. Your self-worth hits the bottom, and a voice inside says, "You're no good." All of this combined makes you feel worm-like. You need reassurance that God did not create you to be a worm, and will not leave you in this condition.

The psalm describes physical and psychological problems: "all my bones are out of joint; my heart is like wax; it is melted within my breast; my mouth is dried up . . . you lay me in the dust of death" (vv. 14–15). Depression causes many physical and emotional problems, physical pain, exhaustion, heartache, and sleeping and eating disorders. All these can make you feel like your bones are out of joint. The dust of death appears to be where you are heading. "Counting bones" (v. 17) may refer to the loss of weight that sometimes comes with depression. But the psalm is not over.

This psalm deals with enemies on the attack. Animals represent the enemy—they are fierce and scary. These wild animals seem to be out to get you; to tear you apart. Who are your enemies? Could the enemy be stress, ridicule, conflict, battles over turf, or loss of a promotion? The enemies could also be voices from within that tell you you're no good; that you can't do that; that you are not important to God. These enemies may tell you that you don't have enough faith, or are not worthy of God's love. These are the false voices of depression. The Scripture tells you something else.

Then the mood of the psalm changes. The writer is going to praise God in the congregation and calls others to do the same. There is reassurance: "He (God) did not hide his face from me, but heard when I cried to him" (v. 24). "He (God) has done it" (v. 31). God has answered prayer. When you cry out, when you plead for

God to help you, and remember God's goodness, praise often follows.

DISCUSSION AND WRITING

Which parts of Psalm 22 spoke to you? Was it the spiritual crisis of abandonment? Or the enemies who are like wild animals? What about the self-deprecation? Did you hear the promise of God's faithfulness? The psalm moves from what seems like abandonment to reassurance that God has not abandoned us but cares and provides.

FINISHING

Pray a prayer offering as much thanks as possible. The words of the following hymn can also be a prayer. You may recognize the words.

Just as I Am, Without One Plea

Just as I am, without one plea
But that Thy blood was shed for me,
And that Thou biddest me come to Thee,
O Lamb of God, I come, I come!

Just as I am, though tossed about
With many a conflict, many a doubt,
Fightings and fears within, without,
O Lamb of God, I come, I come!

Just as I am, Thou will receive,
Wilt welcome, pardon, cleanse, relieve;

Because Thy promise I believe,
O Lamb of God, I come, I come!

Just as I am, Thy love unknown
Has broken every barrier down;
Now to be Thine, yea, Thine alone,
O Lamb of God, I come, I come![5]

EXERCISE 4

PSALMS 42–43: "HOPE IN GOD"

BEFORE YOU BEGIN

Psalms 42 and 43 belong together, so I have grouped them as one. This psalm writer has a deep thirst for God. Apparently, he has become isolated, exiled. He is no longer part of the community of faith and suffers because of this. This psalm speaks to the withdrawal and isolation that often happens with depression. The loss of community grieves people of faith. At our point of greatest need for friends, family, and church, we pull away. When we have lost hope and turned inward, this psalm calls us to hope in God.

BEGIN WITH PRAYER

O Lord, you know me. You know when I am lonely and lost. I feel cut off from all the people that I love. I have lost the feeling of home, security, and comfort. Come to

my rescue. Be my comfort and strength. Show me how
you love me. Show me how you want to end my exile
and bring me home. I trust you, O God. Amen.

<u>READ THE PSALM</u>

"Why are you cast down, O my soul?" becomes a
refrain that always has the same answer: "Hope in
God." As you offer Psalms 42 and 43 to God as prayer,
let them be a receptacle for your hurts, loneliness, and
hopelessness.

Listen for the way the psalm writer turns from the
gloom of exile to remembering the good times in the
community, and how he trusts that once again he will
praise God. Listen. What do you hear? What do Psalms
42 and 43 speak to your life? Is there a new way, a new
understanding, and a new idea of how your life can be?
Listen.

Psalm 42

Longing for God and His Help in Distress
To the leader. A Maskil of the Korahites.

^{1}As a deer longs for flowing streams,
    so my soul longs for you, O God.
^{2}My soul thirsts for God,
    for the living God.
When shall I come and behold
    the face of God?

³My tears have been my food
    day and night,
while people say to me continually,
    "Where is your God?"
⁴These things I remember,
    as I pour out my soul:
how I went with the throng,
    and led them in procession to the house of God,
with glad shouts and songs of thanksgiving,
    a multitude keeping festival.
⁵Why are you cast down, O my soul,
    and why are you disquieted within me?
Hope in God; for I shall again praise him,
    my help
⁶and my God.
My soul is cast down within me;
    therefore I remember you
from the land of Jordan and of Hermon,
    from Mount Mizar.
⁷Deep calls to deep
    at the thunder of your cataracts;
all your waves and your billows
    have gone over me.
⁸By day the LORD commands his steadfast love,
    and at night his song is with me,
    a prayer to the God of my life.
⁹I say to God, my rock,
    "Why have you forgotten me?
Why must I walk about mournfully
    because the enemy oppresses me?"
¹⁰As with a deadly wound in my body,

my adversaries taunt me,
while they say to me continually,
    "Where is your God?"
[11]Why are you cast down, O my soul,
    and why are you disquieted within me?
Hope in God; for I shall again praise him,
    my help and my God.

Psalm 43

Prayer to God in Time of Trouble

[1]Vindicate me, O God, and defend my cause
    against an ungodly people;
from those who are deceitful and unjust
    deliver me!
[2]For you are the God in whom I take refuge;
    why have you cast me off?
Why must I walk about mournfully
    because of the oppression of the enemy?
[3]O send out your light and your truth;
    let them lead me;
let them bring me to your holy hill
    and to your dwelling.
[4]Then I will go to the altar of God,
    to God my exceeding joy;
and I will praise you with the harp,
    O God, my God.
[5]Why are you cast down, O my soul,
    and why are you disquieted within me?
Hope in God; for I shall again praise him,
    my help and my God.

COMMENTS

Have you ever been really thirsty? This psalm compares the soul to a deer who is sniffing out water in a dry desert.[6] There is a longing for the water. The longing in the soul is as deep and as powerful as the longing for water when we are near death from lack of water. That is the way our souls long for God. Just as the body cannot live without water, so the soul cannot live without God.

What is it about depression that numbs the longing of the soul? I wrote in my journal that the world seemed like a dead landscape—nothing was alive. Nothing lives without water. When you are depressed, you might be afraid of falling into nothingness. The longing for God lies underneath the fog, confusion, and terror.

When someone gets depressed, they usually withdraw in two ways. They withdraw within themselves trying to deal with the pain. Because there's no energy to interact with others, sometimes they withdraw from friends, neighbors, and family. Sometimes they withdraw from the church, which has provided their support. Why is it important to go to church? Because in church people pray for you when you can't pray for yourself. In church, people believe for you when you can't believe for yourself. The community of faith can provide support for you while you are depressed. But you need to remember that depression is often misunderstood. For this reason, you should go slow in sharing with the larger group. Begin with a smaller group that you know and trust.

Psalms 42 and 43 ask this question over and over:

> Why are you cast down, O my soul,
> and why are you disquieted
>   within me?

The answer to the problem is to turn to God:

> Hope in God; for I shall again praise him,
> my help and my God.

What does it mean to be cast down? It means to be sad, put low, or oppressed. Each time you ask "Why?" the answer comes back, "Hope in God; for I shall again praise him, my help and my God."

This message of the congregation (Ps. 42:4), the glad shouts, the songs of thanksgiving, the multitude keeping festival—all speak of God to the deepest parts of our lives. And that is the message this person has lost. The psalm writer is in exile, cut off from the Temple and God.

Exile is common in depression. One of the most important things I learned from depression is that we have to be ourselves. Most of us wear masks to disguise our identity from those around us. Perhaps we feel that if they really knew us, they would reject us. If they *really* knew the deep-down stuff, they would judge us incomplete or flawed or something else even more terrible. My problem was that I had cut myself off from whom I really was. I lived in a self-imposed exile from myself and others. I could love others but had difficulty loving myself. I could minister to others, but not myself. I could be accepting and forgiving of others, but not myself. Depression taught me that I had to get to know myself. And learn to love myself. I still am recovering from this—still learning to be kind to me, to love me, to accept me, and to allow myself to be ministered to. The exile was real. I had to come home.

If you can find a community of faith where you feel safe and accepted, it will be a harbor from the storm. This community may be your church, a small group of friends, or just you and your pastor. When I was really depressed, I went to a music and worship conference at a retreat center in North Carolina. One thousand church musicians and pastors were there. Everyone could sing—except me. When they sang, it was like angels. I was brought closer to God as people prayed, preached, and praised God. The week of music and worship renewed my soul. Like a sponge, I absorbed something important—the love of the community.

My journey through depression led me away from the church I served as pastor. There were conflict and hostility in this church. As you may know, it's difficult to make good decisions when you live in a fog bank. The distortion of depression makes you see things that are not there. For some reason that I don't understand, this distortion caused me to take things personally. Misunderstandings and hurt feelings developed over time. When I was well enough to make a good decision,

I decided that the ministry there was too painful for me. It was not a healthy place for my continued recovery. I left people for whom I had a deep love and affection and entered a self-imposed exile. My wife and I moved to the North Georgia mountains where we had a family home. My plan was to take a year off and see what God wanted me to do for the rest of my life. Thoughts of leaving the church altogether crept into my mind. But what would I do? I spent my days hiking and enjoying the beauty of the fall. I began working on a degree at Columbia Seminary. I agreed to preach for eight weeks at a nearby church. Presbyterian Cursillo, a renewal event, provided opportunities for me to minister to others and to find healing for myself. Everything went OK for three months. In January, things got bad. By February, I had a deep hurt inside. It was a yearning— like the deer panting for the water—for the community of faith. I was exiled from the church. I felt like Jeremiah when he said, "If I say, 'I will not mention him, or speak any more in his name,' then within me there is something like a burning fire shut up in my bones" (Jer. 20:9). The psalm writer was in exile, like I was in exile in the mountains. We both were cut off from the familiar "throngs" going to worship. This painful experience renewed my call to be a pastor. Exile is no fun.

A problem pops up in this psalm. You may have experienced the same thing. Perhaps you have said to yourself, "If God loves me, why do I have so much trouble?"

This question has been asked throughout history. The psalm provides the only answer: "Hope in God."

Depression makes you look inside yourself. You focus on the pain inside, and this becomes all you can think about. Survival takes the highest priority. However, you become isolated, with a distorted view of reality. This isolation leads to self-defeating behavior. If you can get outside yourself, it will help. The psalm turns you again and again to God and others. It calls you to end your self-focus type of exile and return to the people you love, who will "speak the truth in love."

DISCUSSION AND WRITING

Share with your group or write in your journal what was important for you in Psalms 42 and 43. Sometimes it is helpful to make a list. What about listing all the things in your life that give you hope? If you can't think of any, don't despair. Later, you may realize that there are signs of hope. Then you can make your list. Or, list all the things, situations, and disappointments that drain off hope. Write them down. Offer them to God in prayer. Tear them up and throw them away. You may discover a new freedom.

FINISHING

Prayer:

> Lord, I want to hope in you but sometimes there is only emptiness. Restore my sense of hope. Let me hope against hope. And Lord, I am lonely, empty, and afraid.

Help me to trust your promises and receive strength from them. Amen.

The following spiritual song has become one of my favorites. The words have power and depth. They speak of a loving relationship with Jesus—one that heals. You may find these words helpful as a prayer or for reflection.

Come to the Water

You said you'd come and share all my sorrows.
You said you'd be there for all my tomorrows.
I came so close to sending You away,
But just like you promised You came here to stay—
I just had to pray.

Chorus:
And Jesus said: Come to the water, stand by my side,
I know you are thirsty, you won't be denied.
I felt every teardrop when in darkness you cried,
And I strove to remind you that for those tears I died.

Your goodness so great I can't understand,
And dear Lord, I know that all this was planned.
I know you're here now and always will be.
Your love loosed my chains, and in You I'm free—
But Jesus, why me?

Jesus, I give you my heart and my soul.
I know that without God I'll never be whole.

Savior, You opened all the right doors.
And I thank You and praise You from
Earth's humble shores—
Take me, I'm yours.[7]

EXERCISE 5

PSALM 77: "IN MY DAY OF TROUBLE"

<u>BEFORE YOU BEGIN</u>

Psalm 77 starts with complaint. There is trouble. Once
again, the psalm writer refers to God turning away. God
has changed. And the writer asks—pleads—for God to
help in time of distress. The shift to confidence comes
when the writer remembers. God's mighty deeds in the
past give reason to hope in the present. Verses 16–20
don't seem to fit. They are more of a poem about God's
power over nature. But what an ending for one who feels
abandoned! "You led your people like a flock by the
hand of Moses and Aaron" (v. 20). God as shepherd
brought the people through the wilderness and provided
for their needs. Will he do less for us?

<u>BEGIN WITH PRAYER</u>

O Lord, in my trouble I forget that throughout time
you have been taking care of your people. Be my shepherd in these dark times. Lead me as a part of your
flock. Protect me from the wolves in my midst. Restore

my health. Give me new life. Help me to remember times in my life when you have saved me, lifted me up, and provided for me. I pray for all people in trouble and thank you that you hear our prayers. Support us all the days of our lives. Amen.

READ THE PSALM

Psalm 77

God's Mighty Deeds Recalled

To the leader: according to Jeduthun. Of Asaph.
A Psalm.

¹I cry aloud to God,
aloud to God, that he may hear me.
²In the day of my trouble I seek the Lord;
in the night my hand is stretched out without
wearying;
my soul refuses to be comforted.
³I think of God, and I moan;
I meditate, and my spirit faints.

Selah

⁴You keep my eyelids from closing;
I am so troubled that I cannot speak.
⁵I consider the days of old,
and remember the years of long ago.
⁶I commune with my heart in the night;
I meditate and search my spirit:
⁷"Will the Lord spurn forever,

and never again be favorable?
⁸Has his steadfast love ceased forever?
   Are his promises at an end for all time?
⁹Has God forgotten to be gracious?
   Has he in anger shut up his compassion?"

                        Selah

¹⁰And I say, "It is my grief
   that the right hand of the Most High
     has changed."
¹¹I will call to mind the deeds of the LORD;
   I will remember your wonders of old.
¹²I will meditate on all your work,
   and muse on your mighty deeds.
¹³Your way, O God, is holy.
   What god is so great as our God?
¹⁴You are the God who works wonders;
   you have displayed your might among
     the peoples.
¹⁵With your strong arm you redeemed your people,
   the descendants of Jacob and Joseph.

                        Selah

¹⁶When the waters saw you, O God,
   when the waters saw you, they were afraid;
   the very deep trembled.
¹⁷The clouds poured out water;
   the skies thundered;
   your arrows flashed on every side.
¹⁸The crash of your thunder was in the whirlwind;
   your lightnings lit up the world;
   the earth trembled and shook.
¹⁹Your way was through the sea,

your path, through the mighty waters;
yet your footprints were unseen.
^{20}You led your people like a flock
by the hand of Moses and Aaron.

COMMENTS

The writer of Psalm 77 is in pain. He says, "My soul refuses to be comforted." The dreadful question, "Does God love me?" comes up in verses 7–9. "Has God changed? Has God forsaken me?" In verse 11, the psalmist turns to the past for assurance. He will meditate, remember, and muse on the holy way of God. "What god is so great as our God?"

Once again, we hear a cry to God. "I cry aloud." To cry aloud is to get it out—to put it into words, groans, sighs, rage. "In the day of my trouble I seek the Lord." Trouble? Yes. Listen to the signs of trouble:

"my soul refuses to be comforted" (v. 2)

"You keep my eyelids from closing" (v. 4)

"I am so troubled that I cannot speak" (v. 4)

Depression impacts eating and sleeping patterns. Sometimes people eat more, sometimes less; sometimes people sleep more, sometimes less. I can remember the days of exhaustion when night after night I wandered through the house seeking relief. For me, nothing can be as hard to handle as these dysfunctions of depression:

eating and sleeping. The good news is that they often respond to medication. Knowing that the illness causes your problems with eating and sleeping can take away some of the fear.

Restlessness, inner turmoil, and weariness go with depression. It is difficult to find comfort. Confused and troubled, it is difficult to speak, concentrate, or organize. When you live in a fog bank, two and two won't go together. When your energy is completely drained, it is difficult to speak or carry on a conversation. Doing so requires too much.

Where does this psalm writer turn when in deep trouble? He remembers God and makes a list of the ways God has helped in the past. If God has helped before, God will help again. If you can remember how God has worked in your life, it will help. Remember how God made you, gave you life, and got you through hard times. Remember how God taught, guided, loved, and supported. Making a list of blessings can be a big help. If possible, pray the list as thanksgiving. The psalm ends with confidence: "You led your people like a flock . . ."

DISCUSSION AND WRITING

If you were to write a psalm, how would it go? Try it. Start with protest, go to petition, and end with praise. Here is a psalm that I wrote in my journal.

O Lord, you have stripped me bare; you brought me to bare essentials—to the place where there is nothing else. And I discovered there—Grace—at the bottom, in the dark—there was grace.

> You have brought me out of the pit
>   of desolation—the miry bog.
> You have given me a rock to stand on—faith;
>   And I know that now.
> I have watched as You have been healing me
>   and I praise you.
> I now have light in my life—it is no longer
>   all darkness.

Joy? Yes, joy is returning! I know now that there will be pain—much pain—in the future, but you are giving me the tools to deal with it creatively and effectively. You are awakening in me "The Song of the Bird." (Thomas G. Lewis 10-28-92)

FINISHING

Rest, and pray: "Thank you Lord. Amen."

EXERCISE 6

PSALM 40: "SINGING A NEW SONG"

BEFORE YOU BEGIN

Psalm 40 begins with thanksgiving. God has delivered this person from illness or trouble, maybe even soul trouble. Verses 1–12 sing praises to God for rescuing him from the "pit." This psalm reminds me of a time in depression when you have partially recovered. Then you can sing a song of praise. But depression is a slippery slope. Trouble still lurks out there. The danger of falling back into the pit remains a constant threat. A lament follows the thanksgiving. Once again, read the psalm slowly, reverently—aloud, if possible. Listen for neon words— words that light up for you. These could be words of trouble or joy. Let the neon words bring light to your inner life. Pause and spend some time with these words.

In reading Psalm 40, you will discover that the psalmist praises God, offers complaint, and ends with a note of confident hope.

BEGIN WITH PRAYER

Thank you O God for the new song in my heart. Thank you for the light that has broken through the curtain of darkness. My life is better. But I feel I'm never far from slipping back into despair. Help me not to spiral downward. Support me O Lord. For you are my God. Amen.

Psalm 40

Thanksgiving for Deliverance and Prayer for Help
To the leader. Of David. A Psalm.

[1] I waited patiently for the LORD;
    he inclined to me and heard my cry.
[2] He drew me up from the desolate pit,
    out of the miry bog,
and set my feet upon a rock,
    making my steps secure.
[3] He put a new song in my mouth,
    a song of praise to our God.
Many will see and fear,
    and put their trust in the LORD.
[4] Happy are those who make
    the LORD their trust,
who do not turn to the proud,
    to those who go astray after false gods.
[5] You have multiplied, O LORD my God,
    your wondrous deeds and your thoughts
        toward us;
    none can compare with you.
Were I to proclaim and tell of them,
    they would be more than can be counted.
[6] Sacrifice and offering you do not desire,
    but you have given me an open ear.
Burnt offering and sin offering
    you have not required.
[7] Then I said, "Here I am;

in the scroll of the book it is written of me.
[8]I delighted to do your will, O my God;
 your law is within my heart."
[9]I have told the glad news of deliverance
 in the great congregation;
see, I have not restrained my lips,
 as you know, O LORD.
[10]I have not hidden your saving help within my heart,
 I have spoken of your faithfulness and
  your salvation;
I have not concealed your steadfast love and your
  faithfulness
 from the great congregation.
[11]Do not, O LORD, withhold
 your mercy from me;
let your steadfast love and your faithfulness
 keep me safe forever.
[12]For evils have encompassed me
 without number;
my iniquities have overtaken me,
 until I cannot see;
they are more than the hairs of my head,
 and my heart fails me.
[13]Be pleased, O LORD, to deliver me;
 O LORD, make haste to help me.
[14]Let all those be put to shame and confusion
 who seek to snatch away my life;
let those be turned back and brought to dishonor
 who desire my hurt.
[15]Let those be appalled because of their shame
 who say to me, "Aha, Aha!"

¹⁶But may all who seek you
     rejoice and be glad in you;
may those who love your salvation
     say continually, "Great is the Lord!"
¹⁷As for me, I am poor and needy,
     but the Lord takes thought for me.
You are my help and my deliverer;
     do not delay, O my God.

COMMENTS

I never say that I have survived depression. Rather, I say I am surviving depression. Psalm 40 demonstrates what it is like to get better but still be aware of the danger. This psalm is most helpful when the depression has lifted and new life seems to be emerging.

This psalm begins with thanksgiving for the relief from trouble. "I waited . . . he heard my cry . . . He drew me up from the desolate pit, out of the miry bog"(vv. 1–2). The pit, miry bog, and Sheol—all sound like the dark place of depression. I can remember the feeling of being in a pit and not able to escape. Here is the Good News: God has heard the psalmist's cry and brought him up from the pit.

"He put a new song in my mouth . . ." The writer has "recovered." He praises God and tells others about God's goodness. In verse 6, the writer proclaims that God does not want sacrifice or burnt offerings. Instead of sacrifice, the writer offers himself as a witness to what God has done in providing help.

Yet he still has trouble. He still seeks God's help to combat enemies of the soul: "I am poor and needy, but the Lord takes thought for me" (v. 17). The mood changes when he proclaims that, "the Lord takes thought for me." The psalm ends with, "You are my help and my deliverer; do not delay, O my God" (v. 17).

When depression lifts, your soul begins singing new songs. But still there is the fear of falling back into the pit. Trouble seems just around the corner. Feeling better may come and go. Staying alert to the signals of depression is important. For me, trouble starts when I get too busy and too tired. Then my thinking gets mixed up. I know it is time to get myself back together and do the things that keep me healthy. My relationship with God, my physical health, and my emotional health are all involved. This psalm reminds me of a person emerging from the darkness aware that he or she must stay alert to the signs and keep all the relationships in good repair. When the fear of slipping back into the darkness emerges, you may try to control it through willpower. "Don't feel those feelings," you say to yourself. But that drives the feelings underground where they are more dangerous. Try to face them. Pray them. Turn them loose.

DISCUSSION AND WRITING

What did you hear in Psalm 40? How is it important to you? Could you turn it into a prayer? Try it. Write out a prayer about the importance of what you heard. It could be a prayer of adoration, thanksgiving, confession, petition, or intercession. Or, it may combine various elements. Don't try too hard to name the type of prayer—just pour out your heart to God. If you are in a group, share your prayers if you are comfortable doing that.

FINISHING

Pray the prayer that you have just written. If the words won't come, use the words of the following hymn as your closing prayer.

I Am Thine, O Lord

I am Thine, O Lord, I have heard Thy voice,
And it told Thy love to me;
But I long to rise in the arms of faith,
And be closer drawn to Thee.

Consecrate me now to Thy service, Lord,
By the pow'r of grace divine;
Let my soul look up with a steadfast hope,
And my will be lost in Thine.

O the pure delight of a single hour,
That before Thy throne I spend;
When I kneel in prayer, and with Thee, my God,
I commune as friend with friend.

There are depths of love that I cannot know,
Till I cross the narrow sea;
There are heights of joy that I may not reach,
Till I rest in peace with Thee.

Chorus
Draw me nearer, nearer, blessed Lord,
To the cross where Thou hast died;
Draw me nearer, nearer, nearer, blessed Lord,
To Thy precious, bleeding side."[8]

EXERCISE 7

PSALM 30: "PSALMS OF NEW LIFE"

BEFORE YOU BEGIN

Psalm 30 is a thanksgiving psalm. It has been called a psalm of new orientation. (See chapter 5 for a discussion of orientation, disorientation, and new orientation.) The writer of this psalm has an awesome re-orientation in life. It begins with thanksgiving because God helped him. He cried for help, and God heard his cry. Singing, praise, and thanksgiving replace darkness and despair. Life has changed for the better, and God has done it! Thanksgiving continues throughout the psalm.

I imagine this as a person who has been healed from depression. This healing brings new life, richer and more wonderful than ever before. As you pray the psalm, listen for the words that reflect the way you feel.

Begin with Prayer

How can I find words strong enough, deep enough, rich enough to express my gratitude to you O God? I have been through the darkness. Light now surrounds me. I never thought I would see light again. But you O God, brought me through. I thank you and praise you from the depths of my heart. Amen.

Read the Psalm

Psalm 30

Thanksgiving for Recovery from Grave Illness

A Psalm. A Song at the dedication of the temple. Of David.

¹I will extol you, O LORD, for you have drawn me up,
  and did not let my foes rejoice over me.
²O LORD my God, I cried to you for help,
  and you have healed me.
3. O LORD, you brought up my soul from Sheol,
  restored me to life from among those gone
    down to the Pit.

⁴Sing praises to the LORD, O you his faithful ones,
  and give thanks to his holy name.
⁵For his anger is but for a moment;
  his favor is for a lifetime.
Weeping may linger for the night,
  but joy comes with the morning.

⁶As for me, I said in my prosperity,
  "I shall never be moved."
⁷By your favor, O LORD,
  you had established me as a strong mountain;
you hid your face;
  I was dismayed.
⁸To you, O LORD, I cried,
  and to the Lord I made supplication:
⁹"What profit is there in my death,
  if I go down to the Pit?
Will the dust praise you?
  Will it tell of your faithfulness?
¹⁰Hear, O LORD, and be gracious to me!
  O LORD, be my helper!"

¹¹You have turned my mourning into dancing;
  you have taken off my sackcloth
  and clothed me with joy,
¹²so that my soul may praise you and not be silent.
  O LORD my God, I will give thanks to you forever.

COMMENTS

Thanksgiving is more than an annual holiday; thanksgiving is a way of life. This psalm reflects an individual's thanksgiving to God for help received. "I cried to you for help, and you have healed me" (v. 2). This is the reason for thanksgiving and praise of God. "Extol" in verse 1 means to raise up, lift up, exalt. Another way to say it is, "I will exalt you, O Lord." Why? Because God:

"has drawn me up" (v. 1)

"did not let my foes rejoice over me" (v. 1)

"has healed me" (v. 2)

"has brought me up from Sheol" (v. 3)

"has restored my life from . . . the Pit" (v. 3)

Then, later in the poem, the psalmist adds to the action of God:

"you have turned my mourning into dancing" (v. 10)

"you have taken off my sackcloth and clothed me with joy" (v. 10)

All of this leads to praise and thanksgiving. Psalm 30 begins with exaltation of God and ends with giving thanks forever.

Are you able to let the words of thanksgiving resonate in your soul? Can you join the psalm writer to thank God and praise God? If you have suffered the terrors of depression and now are better, you can join in with this psalmist in listing the ways God has helped you. Remember that God provides doctors, hospitals, counselors, clergy, and antidepressants to help. Do you feel like singing? What about dancing? That's the mood of Psalm 30.

> Weeping may linger for the night,
>   but joy comes with the morning.
>   (Ps. 30:5b)

How many restless, sleepless nights have you spent weeping? Or sorrowful? Or in despair? But the morning brings joy. This is a poetic way of talking about moving through the darkness to a dawning of new life filled with joy. This word "joy" means to give a ringing cry, or exaltation. To give a ringing cry—what would that be like? Would that be shouting to God how great God is or how grateful and joyful you are to be healed? I think so.

In the middle of the psalm, verse 7 reminds us of lament: "you hid your face; I was dismayed." Next comes a cry for help—a prayer of supplication. This is a prayer seeking God's favor—asking God to turn God's face back toward the one who is hurting. How many times in depression do you feel that God has turned away? How often have you cried out, seeking God's favor?

Verse 11 changes the mood from crying out to dancing and joy. By the way, sackcloth was a common sign of grief or mourning. God has changed the psalmist's clothes—from sackcloth to clothes of joy.

I discovered that *praise* in the Hebrew language can mean "to be a shining light" or "to flash forth light." Isn't that a great way to think about praise? When you truly praise God, you become a shining light that gives glory to God and hope to others.

Let the words of Psalm 30 rest with you. Absorb these words as a sponge might absorb water. Give thanks for the blessings already received and those coming in the future.

Yes, thanksgiving is more than a holiday; it is a way of life.

DISCUSSION AND WRITING

If you are in a group, some of the group may be able to thank God while others may not. This psalm, while a psalm of thanksgiving, also contains a lament. If it's appropriate, read the psalm with the group. Let your emotions soar as you remember the ways God has helped. This would be a good topic to write about. Consider making a list of all the ways you are thankful. Share them with the group if possible. Then pray them together or on your own.

FINISHING

Prayer:

> Thank you Lord for turning my dark nights into bright sunshiny days. Thank you for the promise that you will do that. Help me to learn how to live a life of thanksgiving, praise, and joy. I exalt you O God; I sing and dance because of your grace. Thank you. Amen.

EXERCISE 8

PSALM 131: "A SONG OF TRUST"

<u>BEFORE YOU BEGIN</u>

Psalm 131 has no lament. It seems to be a simple call to rest in God's love. As I recovered from depression, this psalm became very important to me. It follows Psalm 130, which begins with the psalmist crying "out of the depths." Psalm 130 pours pain, sadness, and darkness from the soul. It is intense. After the cry, after you have fought the good fight, run the race, and jumped the hurdles, Psalm 131 offers a resting place. Faith comes down to this simple dependence on God, as you quietly accept your place in God's mothering love. I hope it will mean as much to you when you're battle weary as it has to me.

<u>BEGIN WITH PRAYER</u>

Lord God, I am tired. I have fought the monsters inside and outside. I need a place to rest. Your love calls me home to a place of nurture and love. Allow me now to be quiet and rest in your love. Amen.

PRAY THE PSALM

Psalm 131
Song of Quiet Trust
A Song of Ascents. Of David.

¹O LORD, my heart is not lifted up,
  my eyes are not raised too high;
I do not occupy myself with things
  too great and too marvelous for me.
²But I have calmed and quieted my soul,
  like a weaned child with its mother;
  my soul is like the weaned child that is with me.
³O Israel, hope in the LORD
  from this time on and forevermore.

COMMENTS

Depression is like a terrifying storm on the inside. It drains your body of energy, resistance, and light, and leaves you wasted. Soldiers who fight in a war often come home with depression, anxiety, flashbacks, and nightmares (post-traumatic stress disorder). When you fight depression, you develop some of the same problems as a soldier: battlefield fatigue. When you are winning, getting better, you may feel a need to rest in a quiet harbor. To regain your strength. To let things go by.

Psalm 131 begins with an address, "O LORD." The next words set the mood. Rather than an angry, impatient, "How long?" (Ps. 13), the psalmist says:

". . . my heart is not lifted up
  my eyes are not raised too high;
I do not occupy myself with things
  too great and too marvelous for me."

(v. 1)

What is he saying? "Lifted up" could mean arrogant, exalted, or proud. A positive way to say this is that you are meek. Or you have humbled yourself. "My eyes are not raised too high" means virtually the same thing.

The psalmist does not occupy himself with too great or marvelous things. He is not trying to be a philosopher or scholar but has resigned himself to a simple, live-life-one-day-at-a-time attitude. He is not God. And because of this attitude, he can say: I have calmed and quieted my soul like a child with its mother. That's the way my soul is.

There comes a time in your struggle with life when you learn that:

You are not in charge,

You cannot figure out everything,

You must accept a dependent role, and

You must be quiet, still, and simple to yield life's greatest treasure—spiritual treasure.

This psalm uses a powerful and bold image: the image of God as a mother. The image provides healing and hope. Everyone has seen the peace that a baby has when held close to its mother. A calmness and stillness fall over the child like nothing else in life. And to watch the child fall asleep in its mother's arms sends the message of ultimate peace. This peace comes through dependence and trust that the parent will provide.

As depression lifts, you too can find moments of quiet and calm. These slip in when you understand your dependence on God to nurture and provide. Can you see yourself as a child curled up in your parent's lap? Even if your memories of childhood aren't comforting, think of a young child with her mother. Think of yourself resting in God's love. The warring factions within have declared a truce. The battle may not be over permanently, but for now you trust in God. Be still. Get quiet. Bask in the warmth of this image. It leads you to hope.

DISCUSSION AND WRITING

If you are still awake, talk to others in the group about what this image meant to you. Share around the circle. Some may have been comforted; some not. But share. In sharing, you witness to your trust in God, just as the writer of Psalm 131 witnessed to you.

If you are alone, consider writing what you are feeling after praying the psalm. Are you quiet or still stormy inside? Are you trusting or still feeling you must fight this battle of life by yourself? Can you "let go and let God"?

You may not have arrived at the state of mind of the psalm writer. That's OK. Don't feel guilty if you are not there. Instead, could this psalm be a beacon that shines through your darkness with a promise? You can pray for that—to be able to reach the safe harbor of quiet stillness. Consider writing a prayer about this. Begin with the address: "O Lord." Next, state your true condition (frayed, worried, anxious, exhausted, and so forth). Ask God to help you to quiet your soul. Ask God to help you trust in God's ability to comfort, give strength, and heal. And bring you to rest.

<u>FINISHING</u>

This hymn proclaims hope in a God who has been there for us in the past and will be there in the future. If it helps, use it for your prayer or for reflection.

Our God, Our Help in Ages Past

Our God, our help in ages past,
Our hope for years to come,
Our shelter from the stormy blast,
And our eternal home:

Before the hills in order stood,
Or earth received its frame,
From everlasting Thou art God,
To endless years the same.

A thousand ages in Thy sight
Are like an evening gone;
Short as the watch that ends the night,
Before the rising sun.

Time, like an ever rolling stream,
Soon bears us all away;
We fly forgotten, as a dream
Dies at the opening day.

Our God, our help in ages past,
Our hope for years to come,
Be Thou our guard while life shall last,
And our eternal home."[9]

Conclusion

Depression has taught me more about life, myself, and God than anything I've ever experienced. There are two people whom I greatly admire and had close relationships with during my worst times. They helped me see something that I couldn't see. One was Laurie Johnson, my counselor. She helped me come to the conclusion that I had this dread illness and then began helping me to rework my life story, feelings, relationships, guilt, and sin. Nothing was safe from her. In her pushing and inviting, I finally came to better understand myself. We attacked the illusions and the false self that I had spent a lifetime building up. She said depression is like a warning light on the dashboard of a car. When it comes on, you check the engine and other parts of the car. Something is wrong. She taught me to feel. But I had to deal with all the stored-up feelings, a lifetime of them. I had to grieve the losses in my life. I had never grieved them, just put them in a storehouse. Now the door had been blown off the storehouse and everything came out. Over time, I learned to look at things differently. I learned that I was my biggest enemy in the way I dealt with myself and others. I undermined my own self-esteem, got things out of perspective, took things in a personal way, and gave myself false negative feedback.

The other person was Dr. Ben Johnson, a professor at Columbia Theological Seminary. I had known Ben for many years. During the darkest times, he would meet with me and pray. We prayed the Psalms. At one point in this process, he said, "Tom, one day you'll say that being depressed is the best thing that ever happened to you." My reaction was, "How can he say that when I'm in such deep trouble?" Today, I can say that he was almost correct. It was a painful time of dislocation and struggle. My family, especially my wife, Sebring, paid a big price. Our relationship suffered. In the end, it meant leaving a church and starting over. Although this was the most difficult time of my life, God used it to reshape me. The knife cuts deeply into the wood rotating on the lathe in order to make something beautiful. In my case, it made me more honest about myself. Out of all this, God has shown me a new goal for life—to strive for authenticity.

I must admit that at times the voices of despair return. Sometimes they put me into a downward spiral. But now

I know how to stop the spiral. Sebring is my greatest asset in this area. She will say to me, "You're getting a little strange," and I know that the old ways are trying to take over. But I refuse to go to that place again.

We who are pastors know that God uses broken people. We know that God uses us and people all around us who are broken. We also know that God uses the worst situations to bring something beautiful to life. We deal with people in dislocation everyday. It may be the death of a spouse, a suicide, alcoholism, violence, abuse, divorce, depression. Every once in a while, we have the privilege of seeing God's miracle of rebirth. It's the story of being found by God in the depths. It's the story of the flower growing from the crack in the sidewalk. It's the story of crucifixion and resurrection. It's the story of grace.

Each Easter I use a poem called "Resurrection" by Mary Ann Bernard in a sermon or in teaching. The poem ends with these lines:

> A flower comes. It groans, yet sings,
> And through its pain, its peace begins.[1]

Yes, it groans yet sings and through its pain, its peace begins. That is how depression can be a gift of grace—a rebirth.

May the God of hope fill you with all joy and peace in believing, so that you may abound in hope by the power of the Holy Spirit. (Rom. 15:13)

Appendix A
List of Resources

AGENCIES AND ASSOCIATIONS

American Association of Pastoral Counselors (AAPC)
9504 A Lee Highway
Fairfax, VA 22031-2303
(703) 385-6967
<www.aapc.org>   <stacy@aapc.org>

American Psychological Association (A.Psychol.A)
750 1st St. NE
Washington, DC 20002-4242
(202) 336-5700
<www.apa.org>   <fz6.apa@email.apa.org>

American Psychiatric Association (APA)
1400 K Street, NW
Washington, DC 20005
(202) 336-5500
<www.psych.org>   <publiccom@apa.org>
APA Fast Fax 1-888-267-5400
APA also has state, local, and regional centers.

American Psychiatric Press, Inc. (APPI)
1400 K Street NW
Washington, DC 20005
(800) 368-5777
<www.appi.org>

National Alliance for the Mentally Ill (NAMI)
2101 Wilson Blvd., Suite 302
Arlington, VA 22201
(800) 950-6264
<www.nami.org>

National Community Mental Healthcare Council
12300 Twinbrook Pkwy., Suite 320
Rockville, MD 20852
(301) 984-6200

National Depressive and Manic-Depressive Association
730 N. Franklin Street, Suite 501
Chicago, IL 60610-7204
(800) 826-3632
<www.ndmda.org>

National Institute of Mental Health (NIMH)
5600 Fishers Ln., Room 10-85
Rockville, MD 20857
(800) 421-4211

National Mental Health Association (NMHA)
1021 Prince St.
Alexandria, VA 22314
(800) 969-6642
<www.nmha.org>

State Mental Health Associations. For example:
Mental Health Association of Georgia (MHAG)
620 Peachtree St. NE, Suite 300R
Atlanta, GA 30308
(404) 875-7081
There are MHAG offices throughout the state.

BROCHURES ON DEPRESSION

National Alliance for the Mentally Ill Fact Sheets (numerous
    resources on depression)
Helpline (800) 950-NAMI (6264)

National Alliance for the Mentally Ill:
"Understanding Major Depression: What You Need to Know
    about this Medical Illness" (R005)
"Teenage Depression" (R329)
"Depressive Disorders in Children and Adolescents" (R110)
"What Hurts/What Helps" 4th ed. © 1999
"You Are Not Alone: Finding Help for People with Mental
    Illness and Their Families"
"An Illness Like Any Other"

National Institute of Mental Health:
"Depression"

American Psychiatric Association:
Extensive list of publications; contact for more information.

<u>FOR CLERGY</u>

Association of Mental Health (AMH)
Clergy/College of Chaplains
1701 E. Woodfield Rd., Suite 311
Schaumberg, IL 60173
(847) 240-1014
<cochpln@aol.com>

American Psychiatric Association:
"Mental Illness Awareness Guide: Clergy and Other Spiritual
    Leaders"
"Pathways to Promise"
"Congregational Responses to Mental Illness"
5400 Arsenal St., MS 223
St. Louis, MO 63139
(314) 644-8400

"What Hurts/What Helps"
Joyce Burland, Ph.D.
National Alliance for the Mentally Ill Family-to-Family
    Education Program
4th ed. © 1999

Your denominational headquarters most likely have an
office of health ministries that can provide additional resource
information.

Pharmaceutical companies also provide much helpful information on depression. Ask your doctor about what is available.

AUDIO VISUALS

American Psychiatric Association:
"Depression: The Storm Within"

National Alliance for the Mentally Ill:
"Learning to Live with Bipolar Disorder"

OTHER RESOURCES

Insurance Companies: Some insurance companies provide a toll-free number you can call for advice from a nurse or clinician. They also can refer you to physicians in your area who can help with depression.

National Depression Screening Day Project
1 Washington St., Suite 304
Wellesley, MA 02481
(617) 239-0071
(617) 431-7447 (fax)

OTHER WEB SITES

Christian Depression Pages
<www.gospelcom.net/cdp/info.htm>

McMan's Depression and Bipolar Web

Appendix B
Additional Reading

DEPRESSION

Susan Dunlap, *Counseling Depressed Women* (Louisville, Ky.: Westminster John Knox Press, 1997).

Michael Lawson, *Facing Depression: Toward Healing the Mind, Body and Spirit* (Mystic, Conn.: Twenty-Third Publications, 1990).

William Styron, *Darkness Visible: A Memoir of Madness* (New York: Vintage Books, 1991).

Herbert Wagemaker, *The Surprising Truth about Depression* (Ponte Vedra Beach, Fla.: Ponte Vedra Publishers, 1994).

PRAYER

Richard Beckman, et al, *Face to Face with God: A Guide for Prayer Ministry* (Minneapolis: Augsburg Fortress, 1995). This is a kit on prayer for the church.

Arthur Bennett, *The Valley of Vision: A Collection of Puritan Prayers and Devotions* (Edinburgh: The Banner of Truth Trust, reprint 1995).

John E. Biersdorf, *How Prayer Shapes Ministry* (Bethesda, Md.: The Alban Institute, 1992).

Richard Foster, *Prayer: Finding the Heart's True Home* (New York: HarperCollins, Harper San Francisco, 1992).

Ben Campbell Johnson, *Living Before God: Deepening Our Sense of the Divine Presence* (Grand Rapids: William B. Eerdmans Publishing Company, 2000).

Presbyterian Church (U.S.A.) and Cumberland Presbyterian Church, *Daily Prayer: The Worship of God* (Philadelphia: The Westminster Press, 1987).

Marjorie Thompson, *Soul Feast: An Invitation to the Christian Spiritual Life* (Louisville, Ky.: Westminster John Knox Press, 1995).

PSALMS

Bernhard W. Anderson, *Out of the Depths* (Philadelphia: The Westminster Press, 1983).

Walter Brueggemann, *The Message of the Psalms* (Minneapolis: Augsburg Publishing, 1983).

———, *Praying the Psalms* (Winona, Minn.: St. Mary's Press, 1986).

———, *Israel's Praise: Doxology Against Idolatry and Ideology* (Philadelphia: Fortress Press, 1988).

———, *The Psalms and the Life of Faith* (Minneapolis: Fortress Press, 1995).

James L. Mays, *Psalms* (Louisville, Ky.: John Knox Press, 1995).

———, *The Lord Reigns: A Theological Handbook to the Psalms* (Louisville, Ky: Westminster John Knox Press, 1994).

Patrick D. Miller, *They Cried to the Lord: The Form and Theology of Biblical Prayer* (Minneapolis: Fortress Press, 1994).

$\mathcal{N}otes$

Chapter 1: Depression

1. American Association of Pastoral Counselors, *Pastoral Care of Persons with Depression* (reprint, Fairfax, Va.: 2000), 2.
2. Ibid.
3. American Psychiatric Association, *Diagnostic and Statistical Manual of Mental Disorders*, 4th ed. (Washington, D.C.: 1994).
4. William Styron, *Darkness Visible: A Memoir of Madness* (New York: Vintage Books, 1991), 5.
5. Ibid., 12.
6. Ibid., 16.
7. Herbert Wagemaker, *The Surprising Truth about Depression* (Ponte Vedra Beach, Fla.: Ponte Vedra Publishers, 1994), 54.
8. Styron, 14.
9. Ibid., 15.
10. Frederic Flach, M.D., *The Secret Strength of Depression* (New York: Bantam Books Inc., 1975), 2.
11. Susan H. Greenberg and Karen Springen, "Motherhood and Murder," *Newsweek*, July 2, 2001, 26.
12. National Institute of Mental Health. *Depression*. Publication 00-3561 (Bethesda, Md.: Office of Communications and Public Liaison, 2000), 6.
13. Ibid.
14. Wagemaker, 79.
15. Michael Lawson, *Facing Depression: Toward Healing the Mind, Body, and Spirit* (Mystic, Conn.: Twenty-Third Publications, 1990), 78.

16. Styron, 82.
17. C. Welton Gaddy, *A Soul Under Siege* (Louisville, Ky.: Westminster/John Knox Press, 1991), 26.
18. Ibid.
19. NARSAD Research, *Conquering Depression* (Great Neck, N.Y.).
20. Susan Dunlap, *Counseling Depressed Women* (Louisville, Ky.: Westminster John Knox Press, 1997), 7.
21. Christopher Frost, *Religious Melancholy or Psychological Depression?* (Lanham, Md.: University Press of America, 1985), 189.

Chapter 2: Getting Help for Depression

1. American Psychiatric Association, *Mental Illness Awareness Guide for Clergy and Other Spiritual Leaders* (Washington, D.C., 1997), 7.
2. American Psychological Association, *Depression and How Psychotherapy Can Help People Recover* (reprint, Washington, D.C., 2000). www.apa.org/pubinfo.

Chapter 3: Depression As a Spiritual Crisis

1. Dunlap, 1.
2. Wagemaker, 56.
3. Dunlap, 1.
4. Styron, 50.
5. St. John of the Cross, *Dark Night of the Soul* (reprint, New York: DoubleDay, 1990).
6. Styron, 50.
7. Ibid.
8. Dunlap, 1.

Chapter 4: Finding God in Prayer

1. John H. Christy, "Prayer as Medicine," *Forbes Magazine*, 23 March 1998, http://www.forbes.com/forbes/1998/0323/6106136a.html.

2. Rebecca Levine, "Having Religious Faith Can Speed Recovery from Depression in Older Patients," Duke University Medical Center. 28 April 1998, http://www.dukenews.duke.edu/Med/KOENIG.HTM.

3. John McManamy, "Mind over Matter," *McMan's Depression and Bipolar Web,* article 102, p. 1. http://www.mcmanweb.com.

4. Ibid., p. 3.

5. John Bunyon, *The Pilgrim's Progress* (New York: American Tract Society), 143.

6. Dunlap, 14.

7. Thomas Merton quoted in Marjorie Thompson, *Soul Feast* (Louisville, Ky.: Westminster John Knox Press, 1995), 49.

8. John H. Westerhoff III and John D. Eusden, *The Spiritual Life,* quoted in Rueben Job and Norman Shawchuck, *A Guide to Prayer for Ministers and Other Servants* (Nashville: The Upper Room, 1983), 221.

9. The Program Agency, Presbyterian Church (U.S.A.), *Presbyterian Hymnal* (Louisville, Ky.: Westminster/John Knox Press, 1990), 16.

10. Judith C. MacNutt, "How I Discovered Inner Healing," *Weavings* VI, no. 4 (July–August, 1991): 25.

11. Michael Hollings and Etta Gullick, *Into Your Hands: Prayers for Times of Depression* (Mystic, Conn.: Twenty-Third Publications, 1989), 9.

12. Ibid., 16.

13. Ibid., 18.
14. Wagemaker, 54.

Chapter 5: Praying the Psalms

1. Dietrich Bonhoffer quoted in Thompson, 23.
2. Bernhard W. Anderson, *Out of the Depths* (Philadelphia: Westminster Press, 1983), 36.
3. Ibid., 235–238.
4. Walter Brueggemann, *The Message of the Psalms* (Minneapolis: Augsburg Publishing, 1984), 19.
5. Ibid.
6. Walter Brueggemann, introduction to *Psalms of Lament*, by Ann Weems (Louisville, Ky.: Westminster/John Knox Press, 1993).
7. The psalm writers were almost certainly men. I refer to them in the masculine to be historically correct and to avoid awkward "he/she" language. In doing this I have no intention to be gender exclusive.

Chapter 6: Spiritual Exercises

1. Styron, 16–17.
2. Martin Luther, quoted in James Mays, *Psalms* (Louisville, Ky.: John Knox Press, 1995), 80.
3. Mays, 406.
4. Hollings and Gullick, 13–14.
5. Charlotte Elliott, "Just as I Am, Without One Plea," in *The Presbyterian Hymnal* (Louisville, Ky.: Westminster/John Knox Press, 1990), 370.
6. Anderson, 84.
7. Also known as "For Those Tears I Died," by Marsha J. Stevens. Copyright © Bud John Songs, Inc. All rights reserved. Used by permission.

8. Fanny J. Crosby, "I Am Thine, O Lord," in *Hymns for the Family of God*, ed. Fred Bock (Nashville: Paragon Association, Inc., 1976), 455.
9. Isaac Watts, "Our God, Our Help in Ages Past," in *The Presbyterian Hymnal* (Louisville, Ky.: Westminster/John Knox Press, 1990), 210.

Conclusion

1. Mary Ann Bernard, "Resurrection," quoted in Job and Sawchuck, 144.

Bibliography

Allender, Dan B., and Tremper Longman III. *The Cry of the Soul*. Colorado Springs: Navpress, 1994.

American Psychiatric Association. *Diagnostic and Statistical Manual of Mental Disorders,* 4th ed. Washington, D.C., 1994.

Anderson, Bernhard W. *Out of the Depths*. Philadelphia: The Westminster Press, 1983.

Brueggemann, Walter. *The Message of the Psalms*. Minneapolis: Augsburg Publishing, 1983.

—— *Praying the Psalms.* Winona, Minn.: Saint Mary's Press, 1986.

—— *Israel's Praise: Doxology Against Idolatry and Ideology.* Philadelphia: Fortress Press, 1988.

—— *The Psalms and the Life of Faith*. Minneapolis: Fortress Press, 1995.

Dahood, Mitchell. *Psalms I, The Anchor Bible*. Garden City, N.Y.: Doubleday and Co. Inc., 1965.

—— *Psalms II*. Ibid., 1968.

—— *Psalms III*. Ibid., 1975.

Dunlap, Susan. *Counseling Depressed Women*. Louisville, Ky.: Westminster John Knox Press, 1997.

Fairchild, Roy W. *Finding Hope Again: A Pastor's Guide to Counseling Depressed Persons*. San Francisco: Harper & Row, 1980.

Goldingay, John. *Praying the Psalms*. Grove Spirituality Series, no. 44. Nottingham, England: Grove Books Limited, 1993.

Hart, Thomas. *Hidden Spring: The Spiritual Dimension of Therapy.* New York: Paulist Press, 1993.

Hollings, Michael and Etta Gullick. *Into Your Hands: Prayers for Times of Depression.* Mystic, Conn.: Twenty-Third Publications, 1985.

Job, Rueben P. and Norman Shawchuck. *A Guide to Prayer for Ministers and other Servants.* Nashville: The Upper Room, 1983.

Kim, E. Kon. *The Rapid Change of Mood in the Lament Psalms.* Seoul, Korea: Korea Theological Study Institute, 1986.

Lawson, Michael. *Facing Depression: Toward Healing the Mind, Body, and Spirit.* Mystic, Conn.: Twenty-Third Publications, 1990.

Marty, Martin E. *A Cry of Absence.* San Francisco: Harper and Row Publishers, 1983.

Mays, James L. *Psalms.* Louisville, Ky.: John Knox Press, 1995.

Merton, Thomas. *Bread in the Wilderness.* Collegeville, Minn.: The Liturgical Press, 1986.

Nowell, Irene. "Psalm Therapy." *The Bible Today* 34 (January 1996): 9–14.

Palmer, Parker. "All the Way Down." *Weavings* XIII, no. 5 (Sept.–Oct., 1998): 31–41.

Peterson, Eugene. *The Message: Psalms.* Colorado Springs: Navpress Publishing Group, 1994.

St. John of the Cross. *Dark Night of the Soul.* Reprint, New York: Doubleday, 1990.

Stradling, Leslie E. *Praying the Psalms.* Philadelphia: Fortress Press, 1977.

Styron, William. *Darkness Visible: A Memoir of Madness.* New York: Vintage Books, 1991.

Troeger, Thomas H. *Rage! Reflect! Rejoice!* Philadelphia: The Westminster Press, 1977.

Wagemaker, Herbert. *The Surprising Truth about Depression.* Ponte Vedra Beach, Fla.: Ponte Vedra Publishers, 1994.

Weems, Ann. *Psalms of Lament.* Introduction by Walter Brueggemann. Louisville, Ky.: Westminster John Knox Press, 1993.

Wolf, C. U. "Watchman." In *Interpreters Dictionary of the Bible.* Vol. 4, p. 806. Ed. George Buttrick. New York: Abingdon Press, 1962.

Zenger, Erich. *A God of Vengeance?* Trans. Linda M. Maloney. Louisville, Ky.: Westminster John Knox Press, 1994.